LIFE

AT CLOSE QUARTERS

D0383347

BOOKS BY THE SAME AUTHOR . . .
When the Wood Is Green
New Directions from the Ten Commandments
Deeper into John's Gospel
If I Should Die Before I Live

LIFE

AT CLOSE QUARTERS

THOUGHTS ON
NEW AND GROWING
RELATIONSHIPS

Arthur Fay Sueltz

WORD BOOKS
PUBLISHER
WACO, TEXAS

A DIVISION OF
WORD, INCORPORATED

Library of Congress Cataloging in Publication Data

Sueltz, Arthur Fay.
  Life at close quarters.

  1. Christian life—Presbyterian authors.   2. Family
—Religious life.   I. Title.
BV4501.S829   1982   248.4   82-13645
ISBN 0-8499-2957-1

Printed in the United States of America

For
Stephen Sueltz
Fay Sueltz
Garret Sueltz

Contents

7

Preface

EVERYBODY—NOT ALMOST EVERYBODY, BUT everybody—I talk to has a pain in their family. Even people who don't have families have such a pain: the very fact that they don't have a family! People remind me of porcupines in love—needing one another but frustrated by the anguish and hurt that results from life at close quarters.

Yet I become a person only as I establish myself in a web of relationships with other people. Scientists may tell me objective facts about *part* of me— my personality, but as an entity composed of such parts I only become a person if I am recognized as one by other persons. So families become places

9

where people work at close quarters at creating an environment where every member of the family can reach his or her highest potential.

Something mysterious often goes on between people. Like a match causing another to burst into flame on a dark night, we bring each other alive. I've seen this happen when another person simply walks into a room. Even before she says a word faces light up.

By myself I'm a "Dead Sea." Someone else moves in close to me and all kinds of life suddenly starts to take shape, flutter, and swim. Another person brings me to life. But people can also throw water on my flickering flame. If they don't put it out, they dampen it so that it hardly smolders.

I remember a day when I parked my little Volkswagen as usual and went in to work. When I came out at 5:45 that afternoon to drive home I discovered the battery in my car had given up the ghost and died. I couldn't get a spark of life out of it. Nothing.

A service man down the block came to my aid. I watched him attach the jumper cable to the battery in his car and to the battery in mine. Presto! My little Volkswagen came to life. I had drawn on his power to get my power released. With my motor running smoothly, he removed the cable and went his way. Once the outside power got me started I was on my own.

Suddenly, I see something in this fable's cable. I've seen people sit around assuming life is too far gone. Then along comes someone who touches them with new energy. Life throbs and that person moves out of the blahs of living. A mystery, a secret? Not really. It's just the principle of the jumper cable applied to something more than my Volkswagen. Someone touches me with energy and power long enough to get me going on my own.

Hoover Rupert tells how an honored pastor friend lifted him up off the ashpile of disappointment and defeat. A sure thing had gone sour. The anticipated spot in which to serve had been wiped out. But his friend said, "Look, son, just remember that God has a bigger stake in your life than you will ever know." Rupert never forgot how that man brought him back to life.

So I need people at close quarters to bring me to life. But God also has a stake in my life. If I am only what I am socialized to be, life becomes just a matter of good or bad luck. I need absolutes outside of my situation to which I can respond, and in the interaction between me, the world, and God life takes on meaning. Otherwise the world around me falls into shattered pieces that don't match up.

Life at close quarters means stress. For years I made the mistake of seeing tranquility as the chief end of family life. But if it were, why would God have invented children? God seems more interested in growth, and growth often comes full of stress, argument, and noise.

In an article in the *Los Angeles Times* Auren Uris and Jane Bensahel tell of Harry and Harriet Miller who live in a large city. Both have good jobs, are successful in their work, earn about the same salary, and their marriage is a happy one. Then lightning strikes. One evening Harriet comes home excited: "Harry," she says, "the greatest thing happened! I've been offered a big promotion— Vice President of Communications for the whole company! There's just one thing. I have to stay with the company when it moves." And then she tells him the company is moving their headquarters to another city some five hundred miles away.

Harry Miller's expression turns sober. "Too bad. I guess you told them you can't accept." And the argument begins. Harriet insists that Harry could find another job and that eventually they could both benefit from the move. Harry says he likes his job and feels it holds prospects for him that equal Harriet's promotion. He is accused of being selfish and egotistical. Clearly, these two people are in a tough situation. With the rapid increase of two-paycheck families, conflicts like this are increasing.

New times raise new questions. We dare not fall into the trap of letting the family become a place where we browbeat women back from the liberty with which Christ has made them free.

So in what ways must a woman relinquish her role as wife and mother if she is to take her place as a person in the world outside the home? Some young couples simply agree not to have children. That leaves them both freer to pursue independent careers.

For others, the woman stays at home until her children enter college or at least until they can take care of themselves. Then she attempts another kind of career. Unfortunately, by that time she's middle-aged and finds it a bit late to start up the "ladder of success." And others attempt a kind of democratic marriage. Husband and wife share equally in the household chores and in caring for the children. But they too have a problem. Such an arrangement really means turning the children over to some kind of nursery or day-care center as each goes his or her separate way every morning. But who finds that ideal?

So how can we approach life at close quarters today? A marriage usually signals the start of a new family, and a marriage between two believers signals the start of a Christian family. I have to admit, though, that churches sometimes seem more concerned with weddings than with marriages. They get all tied up in the ecclesiastical requirements and turn a blind eye to the relationship between husband and wife. Yet, according to the New Testament the concept of family goes beyond "two of us against the world." And that's a good thing too, because two of us against the world isn't going to work. After all, marriage involves at least six people—a husband, wife, and two sets of parents. And, according to the writer of Ephesians, a great many more than that. "For this reason I bow my knees before the Father, from whom every family in heaven and on earth is named . . ." (Eph. 3:14).

What on earth does that mean? Well, it means that all human groupings—whether the nucleus of father-mother-children or the network of relatives and friends or the nation or the whole human race—are given the name "family" because one supreme Parent, God himself, called them into being and sustains them. If that's true, then the whole concept of family is not accidental or temporary.

Still, the ideal of a father-mother-children family comes under heavy fire today. Sociologists bombard it with propaganda to the effect that the nuclear family was a stage which we have outgrown. Some call it a temporary aberration imposed on humanity by a church that has now lost its claws.

But people get tired of hearing that and begin to question the assumptions being made. Yet everyone recognizes the pressures under which people today live at close quarters. For instance, nearly all families have been affected by the modern habit of segregation by age groups and the pursuit of their own interests by each member of the family. Television may at times bring families together, but usually it blanks out the kind of stimulating talk to which children of past generations owe so much. And the stresses on the family do not only affect young children. They affect older people who in times past were very much a part of the family circle. I saw a *Punch* cartoon that showed older couples in a rather seedy nursing home. One man leans toward a crony and says, "We stayed together for the sake of the children. Then the little rascals put us in the same home."

Today so many special interests make demands on our time and cause conflict in family relationships. I've seen churches do it. A person does not necessarily become a better Christian by attending a church meeting when he or she is really needed at home.

Now, let's take a look at men and women—not only in themselves, but in their curious relations to each other.

> Since people don't have the courage to mature
>   unless someone has faith in them,
>   we have to reach those we meet
>   at the level where they stopped developing,
>   where they are given up as hopeless,
>   and so withdrew into
>   themselves

and began to secrete
  a protective shell
because they thought they were alone
  and no one cared.
They have to feel they are loved very deeply
  and very boldly
  before they dare appear humble and kind,
  affectionate, sincere,
    and vulnerable.

(Louis Eveley)

When God gets loose in a family where life is lived intensely all the time, he has a unique power to shape personality. Plain living together within the will of God can make a family more at home in this world.

I want to thank several people who have helped and encouraged me in the writing of this book. First of all my wife and best friend, Millie, for sharing this pilgrimage with me. My friend and editor at Word, Floyd Thatcher, who gave me unerringly good advice. Finally, two friends and extraordinarily good secretaries, Sharon Richard and Joan Goddard, who typed and retyped these pages and made suggested improvements which I took to heart.

ARTHUR FAY SUELTZ

LIFE
AT CLOSE QUARTERS

1

The

Way

to

Love

OUT OF THE CORNER OF HER EYE A SIXTEEN-year-old watched her parents as she announced, "Ginny's living with Fred. While she waits for the right boy to come along, she doesn't mind practicing with the wrong one. All the kids have talked about love, sex, and marriage. I've made a decision." Father and mother catch their breath. "I'm going for the first one. The other two are too expensive."

The way of love offers no easy answers. Phil Stone reports from Huber College: "My cynical neighbor says if his wife really loved him she would have married someone else." Or as Archie Bunker says, "The only thing that holds a marriage together is the husband bein' big enough to step back and see where his wife is wrong." Only God knows just how many couples struggle along somewhere between divorce and reconciliation.

But I can't live without love. I can paint a chair or write a book without it, but I can't live without it. So how do we find the way to love? When my daughter took physics, she and I got involved in a conversation about light. I think I know what light is. I can see it coming in the window. I see it in the morning when the sun comes up. I know something about the beauty of light, and I know how it transforms the landscape and even my moods. I also remember in physics classes talking about light as wavelengths and particles. But I have a hard time explaining exactly what light is. And I would have an even harder time trying to describe light to a blind person. Besides, if I analyze light too much, I'm liable to lose it. Yes, in a laboratory I can take a prism and break light into its various shades from the deepest red to indigo. But if I push that too far I tend to lose the wonder and the glory and the splendor of light.

I find I have the same difficulty with the way of love. I can't equate love exactly with what happens to a young man in the springtime when his fancy lightly turns to thoughts of love. So how shall we speak of love? That's not an easy question to answer. A woman once bought a brand new red Volkswagen beetle, and she set out to tour the New England states during the summer. While driving through Massachusetts, she noticed a circus on the outskirts of a small town. Pulling her car into the parking lot she went to see the show. But later when she returned to her car, she discovered the front end was caved in. As she stood dumbfounded, an attendant came up and told her that one of the elephants that was trained to sit on a red stool had spotted her car on the way to his act and sat down on it. But the attendant assured her that the manager already had the insurance forms made out. She could have the car fixed. She found the manager, and he assured her that any garage in town would take care of everything.

So she headed back for the parking lot, got into her car, discovered that she could drive it, and started off toward town. But it was such a glorious afternoon that she didn't feel like stopping at a garage and headed straight on to Boston. As she sped down the turnpike, all of a sudden traffic slowed and she found herself at the end of a five car pile-up. Shortly, the police arrived, set out flares, and began to move the traffic ahead along the shoulder of the highway. After several minutes the woman began to pull slowly around the accident. She had almost cleared it when a highway patrolman pulled her over and said, "Where are you going?"

She said, "To Boston."

"Well," he said, "what do you mean leaving the scene of an accident?"

In a flash she saw the spot she was in and realized that some questions are not so easy to answer. Even though we talk about love all the time, it isn't easy to define or to explain the way of love.

Many people believe they have the answer. In a recent survey 85 percent of college students believed they knew the way to love. Many believed themselves to be in love at the moment while they also recalled infatuation experiences during their younger years. But the only difference between what the students called infatuation and what they now called love was that infatuation happened in the past and love was what they were in now.

Obviously, love goes beyond falling in love. I used to wonder how I'd know if I fell in love. People told me, "Don't worry, Art, you'll know." So I waited for something to hit me out of the blue, a mysterious visitation. I thought love would take hold of me like the measles, and once it hit I would live effortlessly in ecstasy the rest of my life. I remember hearing of a young man who fell hopelessly into this swamp of glandular ecstasy. One afternoon he told his father, "Dad, I think I am going to get married."

His father raised a skeptical eyebrow and asked, "Do you love her?"

"Sure, I love her. When I kissed her last night her dog bit me, and I didn't feel it until I got home."

So often we expect some kind of an overwhelming miracle to hit us from out of the blue, and when that happens we think we ought to give up everything for it. Television dramas infer that a man should give up his wife for it. Certain magazine articles and books say that a woman has the right to abandon her home and children for it. And in our century a king gave up his throne for it.

Obviously, if a person falls for this explanation of love, he will also believe that this mysterious visitation can not only *come* out of the blue, but it can *go* just as unexpectedly. It is out of our control. We can't expect such love to last forever, so let's enjoy it while we have it. And when it is gone, forget it; we can't get a flame out of dead ashes.

However, we're urged not to give up hope, for once one of these mysterious visitations has come and gone another may come. We can be a two-time, three-time, four-time loser: we're not limited to just one episode.

But there is something radically wrong here—

John looks at Jane. He likes what he sees. He says he loves what he sees, and John says he loves Jane. Yet he may simply love what Jane looks like to him. In other words, a young man may simply love his feelings about a girl rather than the girl. He really doesn't love the girl at all, but is in love with his own feelings.

And what kind of person characteristically orients life around love of their feelings? An infant. A baby arrives in this world with a ready-made active love-life entirely devoted to its feelings. It has to if it is to survive. A baby focuses all its energy on satisfying its appetites. The baby doesn't care who suffers as long as it gets what it wants. I know two young parents who both work. They came home one Wednesday night dead tired, fixed a little dinner and stacked the dishes in the sink. Then the phone rang and friends invited them over. Quickly they arranged for a babysitter. They had a great time at their friends' home, but arrived home at 11:30 P.M. more tired than ever and desperate for sleep so they would be able to repeat the cycle the next day. Did their baby care anything about that? At 2:30 in the morning she woke them up for a little food and a little sociability. A baby simply wants what a baby wants when a baby wants it. A baby loves its own feelings.

I don't blame babies for that. After all, they're just babies. Babies are simple get-love creatures.

But if a baby grows up to 6'2" and weighs 180 pounds and still wants what he wants when he wants it, and will sacrifice everything for the sake of gratifying his own feelings, he simply has an infantile love life.

And suddenly the whole idea that love simply hits us "out of the blue" looks infantile. It looks like a child dressed in grown-up clothes with a few Hollywood backdrops making an infantile game out of something profound, splendid, and beautiful.

Obviously love goes beyond that. And yet just as obviously love starts with an attraction. One person feels attracted to another. Who knows what attracts two people? Have you ever looked at two persons on their thirtieth or fortieth wedding anniversary and wondered what in the world attracted those two people to each other in the first place? Yet love begins with some kind of attraction.

Soon, though, love moves from attraction to the nature of wanting to be together. But, unfortunately, wanting to be together is not always the same. If a woman falls in love with her feelings about a man, she wants to possess him. Then when she says, "I love you," she really means, "I love me, and I want you." Sex becomes simply an appetite to satisfy, like thirst.

But let's face it, sex changes things between people. *Playboy* and other advocates of unencumbered sexuality ask us to think of sex as merely a "natural" thing like taking a drink of water. This idea, far from being a simple truth, is really a simple-minded error. William J. Bennett notes in *Newsweek* magazine that "it is an error because sexual intimacy, with rare exceptions, is not a matter of juxtaposition of bodies. It involves people as persons and persons are complex: they have needs, histories and souls. Sex may or may not make a relationship better, but it certainly makes it different." People will not love us when we ignore them and only want the sensual satisfaction they can give us. We tend to resent such exploitation.

Then I know other people who have gone beyond simply living together for what they can get out of each other and have made a contract with each other. They want to live together for mutual benefit. Many of them set up a 50–50 arrangement. At first that sounds wonderfully fair. But as I think about it, I discover that when they say "I love you," they really mean, "I'll love you as long as you love me, but not a second longer! I'll love you as much as you love me but not an ounce more." That's a 50–50 deal with emphasis on the bookkeeping.

So now I have to ask myself: Is it possible to go beyond a possessive or contractual relationship? What would it mean to give myself to another person without trying to make that person conform to what I think she ought to be or do? Suddenly, that question lights up my interior landscape like a flash of lightning on a dark night. Now I see how calculating my love can be. For one brief second I realize that I usually love people if they behave within the limits I set for them.

Furthermore, I find people doing the same thing to me. When I'm at work I can tell by the tone of a person's voice that he has just about reached his limit. So I say something just kind enough to keep peace because I don't want him to explode. And at home I can tell by the tone of my wife's voice that the time has come to fix the chairs on the patio after six months of procrastination.

Yet, surely, love goes beyond the calculated limits we usually set. Love demands celebration, not measurement. People talk about making love as though they could produce something that does not already exist. Surely love begins with wanting to be with a human being, not merely with someone who performs the function of a human being. That could make a husband or wife simply a money earner and sex partner. But, so often these days if one or the other can no longer perform their function, then it's all over.

How many relationships end for this very reason? Men and women head for the divorce court because the other person looks unattractive and his or her erotic "function" no longer clicks. Then they end up looking for a younger partner who can perform the function better. Even though they know they should love people and use things, because of earlier disappointment, they feel safer loving things and using people.

When I first began putting my personal survival kit together, I included one tool among others. I would not give much of myself to anyone, not even an animal. I knew if I did people and even animals could break my heart. But as time went on, I found that such a tool was useful only in building a shack of selfishness.

I saw this point vividly on a recent TV documentary based on life in a primitive tribe in New Guinea. This tribe followed the motto, "Look out for number one," to its logical conclusion. They made it the basic foundation of their social life. No one expected help from anyone else for any reason. No one brought food to starving people. Mothers nursed children up to three years and then left them to fend for themselves. Only a few very old people could dimly remember a time when people occasionally helped other people. Now they just drifted through life—bored, dull, and uninterested in anything except finding their next meal. The TV observer said that in the two years he lived among them he never saw a kind act or a display of affection between anyone, and there were no signs of love—not even between mated partners! No wonder they felt bored. This tribe seemed to lack any meaning in living—no friendliness, no affection, no love—just everyone for himself.

A mathematics of desperation exists today. Everybody wants love but few seem able to find it. Yet, would the idea of love excite me if the power of love did not already exist within me? I doubt it. A child who gets good at loving himself suddenly finds he is able to express love to others. And loving persons create an atmosphere in which others may find it easy to express love to them. This leads me to the truth that the way to really love other people is through a mature love for myself. This goes far deeper than simply loving to have my appetites satisfied. It also brings the realization that I can't get love from people or give it to them. Yet I wouldn't find love exciting if the power of love did not already exist within me. If I were not created in and of love, why would I have a yearning for love? Suddenly, now I realize that love is a process by which I express my deepest nature; it is not a commodity I could give or get.

In the New Testament, John writes, "Everyone who loves is a child of God . . ." (1 John 4:7). Human love reflects something of God, for all love takes its source from God. Anyone who truly loves expresses something of God, even if that person does not acknowledge the God and Father of our Savior, Jesus Christ.

What is God? People give all kinds of answers: the Ground of Being, or Mind, or Beauty, or Energy. But the New Testament says, "God is love" (1 John 4:8). Whatever God does he does in Love. So the person who knows God best is not the philosopher who tries to think through his place in the cosmos, or the theologian who arranges and rearranges ideas about God, or the religious zealot who insists on correct doctrine about God (one's own, of course), but one who loves and to that degree lets God work through him.

I have found under certain conditions I can love anybody. So can you. You may not believe that. But I believe you can. A mother told of her young son who never got along with his younger sister. They fought, scrapped, and just about drove each other crazy. But sometimes the boy had no trouble expressing love for his sister at all. He couldn't act nicer if he had an invitation to a party and she had to stay home. He behaved like a perfect little gentleman if he could go to a movie and she had to go to bed.

Beneath that story lies this profound truth. When I feel overwhelmingly happy, I have no trouble expressing love to anybody. I remember so well when I got my Master's degree after three long years. I had to work part-time and my wife worked full-time. But I finally got it, and then just a week before commencement our first child was born. What a bright time in my life. If my worst enemy had come within a yard of me, I probably would have thrown my arms around him. I just felt so good!

Or possibly you can remember a time you spent long hours or days outside the intensive care ward while a loved one was critically ill. Finally the specialist stops by and says, "He's past the crisis. He'll make it." Remember how the world looked and felt then? The sheer joy and peace of that moment was so great that you could have hugged anybody.

So, now I try to imagine the sheer joy of knowing I am accepted, profoundly understood, and completely loved. The way of love starts there. I am created in and of love. And that releases me to begin experimenting in expressing love to people without calculation, without expecting love in return.

This truth has profound social implications even in our complex world today. It means that our fundamental problems are not so political that we can solve them by state action. Not all social issues have political solutions. When someone asked Mother Teresa of Calcutta what they could do to help make this world a better place in which to live, she responded quietly, "Go home and love your family."

It is this kind of love that dazzled the world when people saw it in the life of Jesus. With all his insight into the evil around him and what it might eventually do to him, Jesus went right on doing the best for every man, woman, and child he met— regardless of their worthiness in the eyes of society. And he never got tired of it.

But Jesus knows how easily I lose heart when I try to care about people like that. So he said one day, "If your brother wrongs you, reprove him; and if he repents, forgive him. Even if he wrongs you seven times in a day and comes back to you seven times, saying, 'I am sorry,' you are to forgive him" (Luke 17:3, 4). Obviously, here Jesus is not talking about someone easy to love or to forgive.

In other places Jesus used words like "rebuke" and "repent" in connection with love. Love requires toughness when dealing with a chronically difficult person. How else could I do my best by him? In our relationships Jesus did not rule out anger and rejection, but he did rule out simply giving up. You recall the familiar chapter in 1 Corinthians where Paul emphasized the fact that love is always patient . . . it is kind and doesn't envy anyone . . . it is not boastful nor conceited nor rude . . . it is never selfish or quick to take offense . . . it doesn't keep score of wrongs or gloat over other men's sins.

That's a tough order. This kind of love takes a lot of faith. The demands of a love that does not quit require the sustaining grace of God from whom that love flows. The more I rely on this God who accepts me as I am, who doesn't demand that I react at a certain level of goodness to deserve his love, and who works in everything for good with them that love him, the more I find myself able to love and keep on loving.

2

Between

Men

and

Women

IF MARRIAGE IS ON THE ROCKS, MOST CALIFOR-nians don't know it. A *Los Angeles Times* poll in the spring of 1980 found an overwhelming percentage of Southern Californians do not regret the adventure of marriage enough to wipe out the whole experience. In the movies a man and woman fall in love and marriage follows as a consequence. But real life works the other way around. The deepest love comes after marriage, not before. Of course, men and women feel powerful romantic attachments before marriage, but commitment produces a relationship of depth and power. So the *Times* found most men and women do not want a divorce.

And while they do not expect utopia, they do feel they have a right to a rich, satisfying experience.

But funny things happen between men and women. In her first year of marriage a young girl caught a juicy cold. "Well, honey," said her husband, "I'm worried about my little sweetheart. You have a bad sniffle. I'm putting you into the hospital for a general check-up and a good rest. I know they serve lousy food, but I'll have your meals sent up from Rossini's. I've arranged it all."

The next year when the virus struck again, her husband said, "Listen, honey, I don't like the sound of that cough. I'll call Doc Miller to come over right away. Now you just go to bed. Be a good girl."

The third year when she began sneezing, he said, "Maybe you'd better lie down. There's nothing like a little rest when you're feeling bad. I'll bring you something to eat. Have we got any canned soup?"

When her nose started to run the fourth year, he said, "Look, Jane, be sensible. After you've fed the kids and washed the dishes, you'd better hit the sack." At her first sneeze on the fifth year, he said, "Why don't you get yourself a couple of aspirin?"

A year later he shouted from the den, "Why don't you just gargle or something instead of sitting around barking like a seal?"

And on their seventh anniversary he said, "For heaven's sake, stop sneezing. What are you trying to do, give me pneumonia?"

Yes, things change between men and women. And not always for the better. Problems seem permanent fixtures, beyond repairing. We so often complain bitterly about having to live with a mate who acts today in precisely the way we found so terribly exciting during courtship. I know a young woman who once found a certain man terrifically exciting, but now she feels disappointed in him. When she first met him, she liked his stability and self-control. People couldn't rattle him. He approached life thoughtfully and sensibly. She liked his practical and objective outlook. With him she felt safe. He would somehow save her from her impulsiveness and the messes she generally got herself into.

But today she feels terribly disappointed. She finds this man cold, ungiving, remote. And he stubbornly ignores her feelings. She describes as shortcomings the same things she once described as virtues! He's just no fun to live with.

And when you ask him how he feels, he'll say, "I once felt like the luckiest man in the world to fall in love with this girl. She seemed so alive. She lit up my life with her wit and energy and enthusiasm. But I can't stand her now. She's impractical and demanding and asks more of me than any man can give. She's never satisfied. And when she doesn't get her way she cries irrationally."

So what does he do? First he tries to be "reasonable." When that breaks down, he will withdraw into one of those "thoughtful silences." And he can't understand why his detachment doesn't calm her down any more than she can understand why he doesn't respond when she screams, "All you do is watch ball games on TV."

Each of course wants his or her own way. And each wants it without becoming vulnerable or having to "give in." How do you get a relationship like that off dead center?

I don't think a dash of adultery will spice things up. In a *Time* magazine article, "The New Morality" in November, 1977, Linda Gams, twenty-five, a teacher who lived with her husband Bob a year before marrying him, said, "Intellectually, I think it's fine to sleep around. But emotionally I'd be very, very upset if Bob slept with another woman. I wish I could be more liberated about this. I always felt I could conquer this until I started living with Bob and got dependent on him. It is a definite split in me."

"A lot of people accept intellectually that their spouse will probably have an extramarital affair," says Joan who was married to a Chicago psychologist who often advocated "open marriage." She took him at his word and had an affair. When he found out, it broke up the marriage. Says Joan: "It's easy to be glib about it when it's not happening to you."

Dr. Sol Gordon, Director of the Institute for Family Research and Education at Syracuse University says, "There is a high moral trend among college students that is influenced by the women's liberation movement. One of their primary interests is falling in love and getting married. That is a new phenomenon. For the first time in history, more people are getting married just for love than for other reasons."

Donald Johnson, psychologist at the University of Colorado, sees a similar trend: "The promiscuity concept is dying out like crazy. People are talking about fidelity. It is a revolution against loneliness."

Apparently, promiscuity produces men and women who are more and more incapable of loving. However emancipated it may sound, each act of unfaithfulness somehow closes the door of real love a little tighter from the other side.

When we get in the neighborhood of sex, we're not on the playground. Sex is like fire. It is powerful, it's wonderful, but it is dangerous. It's dangerous in the sense that we cannot play with it any more than we can play with fire.

Not for nothing do great Christian mystics compare the love between a man and woman with the mystical union of the soul and God. Only when we see sex as great, life-giving, and profoundly creative will we make the effort not to damage its possibilities by cheap promiscuity. After all, you can't "cheapen" what is bad in the first place.

From the first chapter of Genesis on, the Old Testament regards sex as a good gift of God. I can't think of a verse that looks upon sex as evil. In Genesis 2:23 Adam bursts unashamedly into the first love song at the sight of Eve.

It's time, though, to give more thought to the depth and beauty of married love and put less emphasis on the aberrations of sex. So the Bible does not talk about the "what" or the "how" or the "where" of sex, but the "why" of sex. That's the basic question. Why do I have this powerful urge stirring within me? None of the best-selling sex manuals talk about that.

So I listen carefully to Genesis 2:18: "Then the Lord God said, 'It is not good that the man should be alone; I will make him a helper fit for him" (RSV). That short phrase, "It is not good that the man should be alone," tells me that all the beauty of nature is not enough to satisfy the deepest longings of humankind. This falls short of giving people meaning for their existence. Only another human being can do that. So Adam looked up and saw Eve and probably said, "At last, here she is!" How many men have said that ever since?

And from that time on, marriage stands as "the queen of friendships." I know few things so inspiring as two human beings living together and loving each other through all the vicissitudes of life.

I know a young man and woman who fell deeply in love and were married. He gave as much of himself as he understood to as much of her as he knew. That's about as deep a commitment as two people can make. Their relationship grew. They were a beautiful young couple. And then one day while she was driving down the freeway, a truck hit her car and paralyzed her from the waist down.

During the first few weeks her husband reacted with tenderness and compassion. When she came home from the hospital, he made every effort to give her comfort and assurance, But things seemed to cool a bit as the weeks turned into months. And one day the husband noticed that his wife's physical therapist was a most attractive young woman.

Before long he can't help feeling she finds him attractive. They meet for lunch, and after a few luncheons together, they arrange a date at her apartment. The evening of the date he tells his wife he has a business appointment and leaves the house.

As he drives towards the apartment, rain begins to fall. He parks several blocks down the street, walks into the apartment building, and takes the elevator to her floor. But as he walks down the hall, for reasons that he can't explain, he begins to feel uncomfortable. Stopping in the middle of the hall, he turns around and goes back down the elevator and out the main entrance into the street. For hours he walks aimlessly. In his mind he remembers his wife saying once, "Modern laws aren't fair. You men ought to be allowed two wives—one to do all the mending and cleaning and the other to have babies and things like that."

As he wanders around in the rain, he starts arguing with himself. "Why shouldn't I enter into a relationship with this girl I find so attractive? I have normal sexual desires. Should I not do it simply because of some outmoded puritan ethic? Besides even the Bible doesn't cover a case like mine."

Hours later he returns home. The house is so quiet that he can hear the rain dripping off his coat as he hangs it up. He notices light coming from beneath the door of his wife's room. Nancy is still up. Suddenly he feels the need to see her very badly, so he pushes open the door and finds Nancy sitting in her wheelchair reading. Looking up she says, "Oh, Andy, come in. You're soaked."

"Yeah, I know."

"Well, why don't you get some dry clothes and make yourself some hot coffee?"

"No, I just want to stay here for a while and talk with you."

"You didn't go in, Andy, did you?"

It felt like someone had plucked a tight bow string inside his head. "Go in where?"

She ran her hand down his arm and said, "Well, sometimes people know things without anyone telling them. You didn't go in, did you? You probably walked up and down the street in the rain. You may have looked up toward her window, but you didn't go in."

For the first time in weeks the young man relaxed. "No, I didn't go in."

"Why, Andy?"

But how could he put that into a sentence or two? How could he tell her everything that had gone on inside of him as he walked out there in the rain? So he simply said, "Because I love you, Nancy. And I've decided we have to get a new nurse."

I believe that kind of struggle for inner integrity helps men and women keep their relationship on course. Yet I know many frustrated people who just head for the divorce court. And I know of situations so bad that divorce may be right, not because it's good, but because the alternative is so bad. But I can't help feeling that it is never the first or second or third, but always the last resort. It is kind of a sad concession that a relationship no longer exists.

It is important to remember that a relationship doesn't have to be perfect to be happy and creative and lasting. I know a man who toasted his wife on their twenty-fifth anniversary with these words, "Honey, through all these years I have carried you safely over the rough places of life, haven't I?"

"You sure have. You didn't miss a single one," she replied.

No, the marriage relationship doesn't have to be perfect to be creative, fulfilling and lasting. It should go beyond a contract people make or break at will and become a relationship full of mystery— a mystery not subject to revision or to an experiment you can abandon when the going gets tough. It is as futile to attempt an explanation of the mystery of marriage as it is to try to explain the mystery of beauty or music or truth. It defies rational explanation and is beyond the paralysis of analysis.

We resist this truth, though, because we are fearful of the unknown. Even nature abhors a vacuum—there's something in the nature of things that tends to fill up empty space. And something about me abhors the unknown. I like to fill up the empty places in my head with knowledge. We have an urge to know and explain everything. I remember an old-time preacher who stood up, opened the Bible, and read a very cryptic passage no one could really understand. Then he closed the book and began his sermon by saying, "Brothers and sisters, this morning I intend to explain the unexplainable, to find out the undefinable, to ponder the imponderable, and to unscrew the inscrutable." Over the years I've read a lot of books on marriage and love that try to do just that—to unscrew the inscrutable. It all seems very right, but on the other hand it could be very dangerous and very wrong.

Keats said of his friend Dilke, "He was a man who didn't feel that he had a personal identity until he had made up his mind about everything." I have that tendency. So it does me good to ponder Keats' comment on the source of Shakespeare's genius: "negative capability"—the ability to live with mystery without any irritable desire to have everything wrapped up and explained. So rather than trying to explain this mysterious element loose in men and women I would rather think with you about it. We need to develop a capacity for mystery in a world we do not understand, for it is in such a world men and women enjoy life not simply because they are known, but because they are not known.

This mystery loose in human nature amazes me. I stand in awe before it and am suspicious of anyone who assumes we could get rid of it by assembling facts. But I find that my sense of awe does not end as I learn new facts, for the greatest mystery is that I can understand at all. So I try to take an open stance toward people rather than a closed one. I find that I can understand and know them better as I open up myself to them instead of making demands on them.

Theodore Parker Ferris points out that mystery always surrounds any human given. Take intelligence, for instance. I didn't ask for it. I might have gotten through life easier without thinking about things. I hassle so many things simply because I can think. I received a mind whether I wanted it or not. No one asked me how intelligent I wanted to be. Who knows why some of us are so smart and others so stupid?

I find human sexuality filled with mystery. I didn't choose to be a sexual being. I didn't ask for it. I didn't work for it. I am one whether I wanted to be or not. No one asked me if I might prefer to live life without this particular complication. Furthermore, I had no choice about whether I would prefer to be a man or a woman.

So mystery clothes what goes on between men and women because we did not ask to be the kind of beings we are. We did not choose it and we may not always like it. Yet a man and woman committed to each other achieve a bodily communion, an emotional communion, and a communion of spirit. It involves a physical union which expresses and creates a much deeper union—the integration of two lives. Two people melt together in a physical act in a way they could never have been joined otherwise.

Yet I know people who are afraid to enjoy sex. Somehow they grew up with the idea that if you enjoyed anything it was wrong. On the other hand I know people who want to enjoy pleasure but refuse to accept the responsibility of the purpose of sex. If pleasure completely takes over a relationship, we're in for trouble. I don't know why, but it just works that way. When I see a gourmet making a glutton of himself, I see a person on the way downhill.

Love gets loose between men and women who dare to share their interests and their disappointments and their joys and their worries and the housekeeping and the children and the bright moments that come into their lives. A love like that doesn't turn sour when they hit a rough place. They don't run from each other, and they don't try to reform each other. They refuse to bury their grievances but insist on bringing them out in the open and work through them. They refuse to go off on tangents of personal abuse.

Let's face it, every argument has its apparent causes. Arguments usually appear to be a conflict of ideas about politics or children or money or opinions about this or that. But behind all the apparent causes of conflict lie the real causes. And the real causes have to do with jealousy, fear, self-interest, and lack of sincerity. So when conflict erupts, I try not to worry about right or wrong too much. I'm better off if I apologize quickly even if I think I'm right. After all, we have to give the people we live with a chance to be ornery once in a while. But it is extremely important that we try to end the conflict on some constructive note. Perhaps we'll agree on concrete steps that each of us can take to resolve the issue. But if quarreling becomes chronic, don't wait until it kills the relationship. Look for help with the awareness that two people who are determined to work through the things that bother them will succeed and then move on to a stronger relationship.

Somewhere I read, "I love you not only for what you are, but for what I am when I am with you. I love you not only for what you have made of yourself, but for what you are making of me. I love you for passing over all the foolish weak things that you can't help seeing in my heart and for drawing out into the light all the beautiful longings that no one else has looked quite far enough to find. I love you because you are helping me to build of the lumber of my life not a tavern, but a temple and out of the works of my everyday not a reproach, but a song. I love you because you have done more than any creed could have done to make me happy. You have done it without a touch, without a word, without a sign. You have done it by just being yourself."

3

When

There's a Father

in the

Family

I HAVE ALWAYS TAKEN FAMILIES FOR GRANTED.
And family means father, mother, and children
living together at close quarters.

I never thought the strain of family life might
forecast its gradual disappearance. But there are
those today who urge freedom from the responsibility of bringing children into the world, and certainly, high rates of inflation lend weight to such
arguments. Yet Martin Marty in the June 1980
issue of *Context* notes Duke professor William H.
Willimons' report on a conversation with a col-
league whose wife was expecting a baby: "Well,
you two are in for some changes I suppose." His

friend responded, "Changes? You couldn't dream of how many changes we're having to make. My whole life is being rearranged by a person I haven't even met yet!"

But in a more reflective mood, the prospective father added, "You know, I never really knew how selfish I was. Not materially selfish—just self-centered, self-directed. I had everything all planned out just the way I wanted it. My wife and I were proceeding down our separate tracks. Now the baby is coming, and there is no telling what we will be learning next."

And Willimons comments, "There is no telling. For nothing so disrupts our tidy futures and nothing so clearly mirrors our human best and our demonic worst. Nothing so demands from us or gives to us as the blessed burden of a child." The 2:00 A.M. feeding is a good test. Or the diaper days. Or the terrible twos and the frantic fours. I know people who try to raise children on the basis of their own personal convenience. Yet surely love means accepting the inconveniences that children bring into the pattern of life by day and by night. Children are burdens which can be blessings.

Willimons suspects that many couples' reluctance to bear children *may* be expressed as an act of responsibility (to world population), but is actually "an untrusting anxiety which results in an overwhelming need for security," or even selfishness. And the question, "Can I, with the world in the shape it is, responsibly bring children into this kind of world?" has to be rephrased, "Can I, with the world in the shape it is, responsibly *refuse* to bring children into this kind of world?"

So the Duke University professor wonders whether we have not overstressed marital terms like relationships, freedom, self-fulfillment, and joy while forgetting the long-standing virtues and roles of sacrifice, responsibility, and vocation. Yes, children make demands. *Esquire's* 1974 pre-inflation conception-through-college cost estimates were $188,941 for boys, $200,691 for girls. We may have to double that soon. That figure has been inflated considerably since then and will doubtless continue to increase.

Because I am a father, I liked columnist Art Buchwald's check on an average father's reminder pad. He discovered these "don't forget to do" memos on his pad:

"Check with the insurance agent to see if any insurance company in the United States will issue a policy to Ellen after she was cancelled by State Farm following the last automobile accident."

"Phone Mr. Barnes at the bank and explain that you will make good on Lilly's overdraft of the check she wrote for the new camera she gave me for Father's Day."

"Call Mr. Swearington and explain to him why

you don't think it would be a good idea for Lilly and his son to go on a two-week camping trip to the mountains."

"Tell David he can't have a party at our house while we are away next week; blame his mother."

"Write to USC and ask them if they will refund half of David's tuition since he dropped out in January."

"Try to get the company to send you on a business trip to Europe for the better part of the summer."

Now, all of us grew up in some kind of a family. Families take many forms. Some families have two parents, others have just one parent. Some families are headed by a guardian or grandparents or an aunt or an older brother. Some families include children, others do not. But all family members affect each other.

In some families relationships just drift with no apparent direction or purpose. Others seem to move toward objectives they hope to reach together fully aware that times and family structures can change with the addition or subtraction of a member. Such changes mean a reordering of priorities and offer the opportunity to discover new directions which will fortify us against the disruptive forces loose in society.

I remember a young man and woman who got off to a shaky start. He wondered about breaking their engagement from the beginning. She was pregnant, and he knew it wasn't his child. Worse yet, political upheaval forced them to take their baby and get out of the country as fast as they could. For years they lived as refugees. Later, when they returned home, they thought their teen-age son had run away. When they found him, his mother asked, "Why did you do this to us? You worried us sick."

And he answered, "Why did you worry about me? Don't you know I've begun to develop my own ideas about who I am and what I'm going to do with my life?" Yet it was this family that knew the stress of early marital conflict, the pressure of a political and economic situation over which they had no control, and the reality of the generation gap that produced Jesus of Nazareth.

A father plays an important part in any family. So does a mother. I didn't choose my father or my mother. Yet, living with them did shape my life. In turn, I have never found it easy to be a father. No one asked me about my fitness as a parent before I assumed the role, and by the time I learned how to relate to my ten-year-old daughter, I discovered she was sixteen.

I find my role as a father to be very complex; I have a responsibility to be male, husband, father, taxpayer, home owner, tenant. Sometimes I'm the authority, other times I'm supervised, and I struggle to carry out my obligations in these many difficult roles. Sometimes I find myself in a position I don't believe I can possibly fill. But, as a father I have to take certain risks, and I have to tolerate some frustration.

The other day as I started out for my early morning jog, I caught my toe on a cracked piece of cement which sent me gyrating foolishly down the sidewalk as I tried to avoid a fall. I felt like turning around and kicking the piece of sidewalk that tripped me up. A two-year-old might have done just that, but I've learned that not all sidewalks are smooth. We fathers have to take frustrations, large and small, in stride.

As W. B. J. Martin once noted, "I remember living with three different fathers. They all had the same name. They were all the same man, but not to me. As a seven- or eight-year-old, I idolized my father. To me he looked like the strongest, smartest man around. He was certainly smarter and stronger than any of the other dads I knew."

I read once about a great opera star who got laryngitis on the night of the performance in Chicago. The hall was sold out, and when the audience heard the announcement that the great singer couldn't sing, they became very angry. His understudy had the unenviable task of singing the lead role in the opera that night. Well, the curtain rose, and the understudy stepped on stage and filled the hall with glorious music. He sang magnificently,

flawlessly, through the whole first act. But when
the curtain came down, even though he sang so
well, no one applauded. They just sat in sullen
silence.

And then all of a sudden from one of the boxes
over at the right you could hear one pair of hands
applauding. Every eye turned to see a six-year-old
boy standing on his seat calling in a loud voice,
"Sing it again, dad. Sing it again. You sounded
great. Sing it again." The mood of the audience
was changed by one boy who idolized his father.

And as a seven- or eight-year-old, I felt the same
way. But when I grew up into my teens, I began to
notice that I lived with a second kind of father.
Dad didn't sound like quite the authority I had
thought he was. I wouldn't go as far as Mark Twain
to say that, "When I was twenty my father was so
ignorant I could hardly bear to talk to him." But a
communication gap had developed. I felt different
about myself and about him. Now, I wish I had just
let dad be dad, but at the time I couldn't. I was too
immature to realize that since I had never felt I
had to deserve his love, there was no reason for
him to have to deserve mine.

But then remember that Mark Twain also went
on to say, "When I was twenty my father was so
ignorant I could hardly bear to talk to him, but
when I turned thirty, he seemed to have learned a
few things. And when I reached forty he'd come

quite a long ways." So later in life I lived with a
third kind of father. No one who is sixteen has ever
been forty, but everyone who is forty was once
sixteen. How easily that fact escapes the notice of
adolescents and their parents. Although the world
has changed in twenty-four hundred years, the
perspective of a sixteen-year-old today remains a
lot more like the perspective of a sixteen-year-old
in the time of Socrates than it is like the perspective of a forty-year-old today. Throughout history
people must learn certain things from experience.
Some of this can be passed on to the young, but
that only happens if the forty-year-olds will speak
of their experience and the sixteen-year-olds will
listen. And no sixteen-year-old will listen unless
someone makes the effort to get his attention.

So after I went through the pain and trauma of
adolescence and early adult life where I struggled
with my own feelings and values and direction in
life, I tended to get a new perspective on my parents and entered into a new relationship with
them. I discovered that a family exists as a kind of
tiny moral cosmos. Families become a place where
people say, "This is how we will live together."
And they say to the rest of the world, "Do your
worst, but here we stand. This is how we will live."
And while we as families live in a world of conflict-
ing values, we can determine our own life style.

Imagine stepping into a time machine, shifting it

into reverse, and sending ourselves back nineteen centuries to a Galilean home and listening to young Jesus and his brothers talking to Joseph. We'd hear them refer to Joseph as "Abba." The word means "Father dear," and it appears only once in the New Testament in the prayer of Jesus in the Garden of Gethsemane. Yet apparently, Jesus used this Aramaic family word regularly when he prayed, and he shared this secret of God's fatherhood only with his disciples. It was the deepest and last secret of his relationship with God.

Centuries earlier Plato wrote: "To find the Maker and Father of the universe is a hard task, and when you have found Him, it is impossible to speak of Him before all people." Jesus seemed to feel the same way. He found in God's Fatherhood a spiritual experience of unparalleled depth. It wasn't something you shouted from the housetops, but something you talked about privately with close and trusted friends. To them he said, "To you the secret of the kingdom of God has been given" (Mark 4:11). What secret? The secret that the King in this kingdom was a Father, the "Abba" of his prayers. Only after Easter did Christ's secret become an open secret to his followers.

I remember seeing "The Caine Mutiny" at the Ahmanson Theatre in Los Angeles. In the novel, *The Caine Mutiny*, Herman Wouk has one of the characters, Willie Keith, receive a letter on the

Caine, a minesweeper. The letter came from his father who was dying of an incurable disease. His father offered three bits of advice to his son:

> "First, there is nothing, nothing more precious than time. Wasted hours destroy your life just as surely at the beginning as at the end. Second, religion. I'm afraid I haven't given you much, not having much ourselves. But I think after all I will mail you a Bible before I go into the hospital. Get familiar with the words. You will never regret it. I came to the Bible as I came to everything in life; too late. Third, Willie, think of me as I might have been at the times in your life when you come to crossroads. And for my sake, and for the sake of a father who often took the wrong turns, take the right ones. Be a man, son.
>
> Love, Dad."

Slowly it dawns on me. The essence of fatherhood lies in its sense of responsibility. I remember the story of the Prodigal Son. The boy reached a point where he said, "I am no longer worthy to be called your son." Civil law might even agree with him. Yet even if the father had no legal reason to take charge of his boy, still an indissoluble bond remained. The father felt compelled to cry out, "My son!" The mystery of fatherhood lies in the exercise of this responsibility without ever trying to evade it.

A responsible father tries to prepare men and women to take their places in an adult world. This

goes beyond pampering and protection. It means
the education of mind and spirit so that each child
feels ready for life. "You must endure it as discipline: God is treating you as sons. Can anyone be a
son, who is not disciplined by his father?" (Heb.
12:7). How easy to romanticize God as the giver of
gifts and provider of protection and security. Yet a
father who makes this the beginning and end of his
fatherly role fails in fulfilling his responsibility. I
spoil the meaning of God's fatherhood and lose
sight of its relevance for my own if I divorce it from
the element of responsibility.

A father has a chance to help create the kind of
moral cosmos that will prepare his children for life
in this dangerous world. I've talked to many young
people with terrible self-images. They don't feel
they amount to much. An article in *Developmental
Psychology Today* noted, "Put the personality of
a child in the body of an adult, furnish a need to be
loved and a fierce desire to be independent, allow a
need to be self-directed but leave out any idea of
what directions to take, add an enormous amount
of love, but also the fear that it may not be accepted or returned, give physical and sexual powers
without any knowledge or experience of how to use
them—take these and place them in a society
whose values and achievements are essentially in-
comprehensible and certainly unattainable and
whose concerns are seemingly misplaced and in-

sincere, then you will have just begun to scratch the surface of adolescence."

At the point of a young person's self-esteem fathers have an important part to play. As a father, I have a chance to help my children believe in themselves. If my children feel secure in my love, they have a foundation upon which to build their self-esteem. They can develop faith in what they may become.

So I try to watch what I tell children about themselves or what I expect of them. I concentrate on what they do well. Concentrating on what they do badly and trying to improve that doesn't help much. No amount of practice will make a great singer out of a tone-deaf person. But a person can greatly improve what he does well. As a young person develops faith in himself, he or she can rise above fear and take chances on a new venture.

Here again, fathers can help by praising the new and innovative and not rejecting novel ideas. I think young people learn creativity when they see father or mother willing to risk. If I have the attitude of "make new" rather than simply "make do," my children catch a basic spirit and learn to step out into their own special way of doing things. After all, no two people work in exactly the same way. Sometimes it helps to brainstorm with young people and watch how one idea triggers another.

In addition, fathers can help young people grow

and develop in their sensitivity to life. I do this by telling them how the world looks to me and how I feel about it. As much as I'm able, I try not to hide my sense of awe or my pain or my enthusiasm. Why should I feel embarrassed if my children see me in tears? Such moments give them a chance to practice giving comfort. They repeat back to me the times I took them up in my arms and brushed away a tear. Sensitivity will deepen the lives of my children in a hundred ways. Yes, they may feel the pain of life more deeply, but that pain may motivate them to do something in meeting the needs of the world.

I hope my children have fallen in love with life. I hope they've caught some of my enthusiasm for it. If they have they will expect it to be interesting and full. One thing I learned right at the start as a new father—children take time. They take time not just as babies and toddlers but right on through the years. Some psychologists say children need the involvement of mother and father more than ever in adolescence and young adulthood in order to mature. If a young person cannot find involvement within his family, he will look for it outside.

This means that a father can invite the involvement of his children in *his* life in a way that fits their age. I now find myself talking with my grown children about my job, about my hopes for the future, and how I plan to invest what money I have. In these conversations I am giving them myself.

Paul Tournier once commented, "Let us not underrate the joy of giving or the joy of receiving, for these are indissolubly related, and both symbolize the joy of being loved. Men need to give because they need to give themselves, and all their gifts are signs of that deep-seated and universal desire to give oneself. To love is to commit oneself."

Children learn values, and each generation of adults must make an effort for each generation of children to help them understand their spiritual inheritance. That inheritance may be their birthright, but it does not come with birth. Free, thoughtful, responsible people do not happen naturally or by accident. Such people emerge as the result of the intensive effort of fathers and mothers. It means fathers and mothers must consciously support institutions and conditions that move civilization along and provide new participants in it.

So, a father can try to assure his troubled child that no matter what happens in life in the way of success or failure he will always be welcomed to the party. The music plays for him too, if he will listen and move his feet.

Above all, I, as a father, can let my children know I love them. I can stroke their hair and hold their hands. I can let them know how valuable I think they are and how important they are to me. And I can let them know how important I believe they are to the whole scheme of things. Then I can let them know how much poorer my life would have been if they had never come into it. And I hope they will forgive me if I ever compared them unfavorably with anybody else, or played down their abilities.

And, finally, I can let my children know that if they do certain things that they are free to do, they may make shipwreck of their life. I must help them understand that there is something about the spirit of humanity which suggests a greater grandeur and mystery of life in this universe—there is a spirit greater than human loose in the world that is creating an extended family of the young and old, married and unmarried, divorced and widowed, religious and irreligious—westerners, easterners, happy people, miserable people, lonely people, gregarious people. There is a Father in the family.

4

A

Woman's

Place?

HOME CAN MEAN A TOUCH OF HEAVEN OR A TASTE of hell. Sometimes both. Most of the time neither. It serves as a miniature of life lived at close quarters. And what about the woman's place? Who can deny that the role of woman has changed in the last generation? The women's movement opened up new opportunities for women to fulfill themselves outside the home. Today women can earn more money and have a wider selection of careers than ever before. Women with talent and brains and ability win recognition in almost every area of today's society. But some women I talk with sense that they may have paid a steep price for these opportunities without realizing it.

Candice Bergen in a July 24, 1977, interview in the *Los Angeles Times* comments, "When a woman turns thirty her life becomes a soap opera." She says she suffers from excess liberation—as much a victim of the feminist movement as its beneficiary.

What's more, she says she is not alone. The reporter, Bettijane Levine, goes on to quote her:

"There is a whole group of people my age, the atomic babies, who grew up with no faith in anything at all. We lived just for the immediate moment, spent our teens and twenties disencumbering ourselves from traditional values, making ourselves what we thought was free. Now we realize that maybe what we've done is give up the things we really wanted most—the possibility to have children and a family life.

"Don't get me wrong. I think the women's movement was crucial and valid in all the basics. But it ignored some emotional and biological realities. And that part of it was dangerous and destructive. After all, there are only certain times in your life when you can have children and build a family.

"So I'm now wondering if all this liberation should be re-evaluated. I mean, five years ago I thought the most courageous thing was not to get married, not to have children. That all seems so predictable and safe.

"Now I think the most courageous thing is to get married and *have* children, because that is the most worthwhile—if not the most impossible thing—to try for. There are certain age-old realities you can't refuse. You can modify them and try to make them more intelligent, which is what the women's lib movement basically did. But in the process, a lot of people got dehumanized."

And what about motherhood? Apparently even primitive humanity lived in a family. The April 1979 edition of the *National Geographic* described footprints of a man and a woman walking together that had been covered for three and a half million years by volcanic ash. The pictorial recreation of the scene showed the woman carrying a child. The article suggests that even our prehistoric ancestors lived in families.

Have you ever stopped to wonder why we call nature "mother nature" and the earth "mother earth"? There's something about such phrases that ranges from the light-hearted to the profound. Yet many fail to see the distinction between maternity and motherhood. Most of us seem to take for granted that the two mean the same thing. But they don't mean the same thing at all. Maternity goes back to the origins of nature. Giving birth. Motherhood has to do with the humanizing of life. Maternity describes a biological fact. Motherhood describes a spiritual reality.

Children construct their picture of the world largely through their experience with their mothers. If a child feels mother love, he or she will feel a part of a loving world. Endowed with all the necessary drive to develop as a human being, a child learns to love by being loved. When children are not loved, they fail to learn to love. And as unloved children grow up, they find it very difficult to understand the meaning of love and are likely to jump into all sorts of shallow relationships.

A few years ago James Reston, the distinguished journalist and vice-president of the *New York Times*, wrote about his mother: "Having found very few answers among the great men of the world, I have been interviewing my mother recently about the pointless miseries of the human race. I think she is news because unlike most mortals she has never been plagued by doubts and the older she gets the surer she is of her answers. I should explain. She is ninety-four, lives in Santa Cruz, California, and is in almost good enough shape to play tight end for the L.A. Rams. Her view is, 'All this "progress" is merely a wickedness going faster.' She always knew that life wouldn't be a daisy and the trouble now is that people expect too much and deserve so little. The great thing about Calvinism, she thinks, is that you expect so little that you are always ahead of the game. On more mundane questions she has equally strong convictions. For example, she is not at all in sympathy with the women's liberation movement.

They don't go nearly far enough for her. She doesn't want equality for women, but authority. Most men in her view are spoiled and willful children who will go to the bad unless policed by some good woman."

Yet surely the humanizing of life offers today's women a great opportunity. I grew up taking for granted that older people cared about younger people. I assumed my parents would take care of me. But the world did not always work that way. In fact, as late as the third century, a mere seventeen hundred years ago, parents simply discarded a child if they wanted to have a more active social life. They just took the baby out to the city wall and abandoned it. That sounds incredible today. Today we take kindness, not cruelty, for granted. We take support, not neglect, for granted.

Gene Stinson confessed recently in a letter published in *Faith at Work* magazine, "As a mother I yelled and spanked in what seemed a hopeless effort to make our daughters 'good' because perfectly behaved children are a credit to their parents. Frank and I were quite vocal in our relationship, each of us fighting for the last word.

"Very often we screamed divorce. Only a lack of courage and a mountain of pride bound us to each other. Neither of our families had ever had a divorce and we were not going to bow to failure. If you have ever seriously considered divorce you know that it is not an easy thing for responsible people. Besides marriage provides a certain security even in the absence of happiness, where only fear or selfishness hold the 'now' firm. Tugging at one's heart strings, too, are a host of shared experiences of loved ones, memories, financial success or woe, good times you have shared or concerns over children . . . . People liked both Frank and me and I couldn't shake the feeling something must be terribly wrong with me if I couldn't do better in my relationships to him and my children. I was coping, but some of the problems seemed permanent fixtures, quite beyond repairing."

It may sound simplistic to say it, but all women who marry and become mothers have difficulties. However, the number of problems is less important than the expectations a woman and a man brought to the marriage in the first place. Women who have excessively romantic and unrealistic ideas about how happy their man or children will make them seem doomed from the start, and the same applies to those who see sex as their chief means of communication.

Yet a woman can surely aim at nurturing the spirit as well as the body of her child. Of course, in the process she may miss not only the bulls-eye but the target. But that happens when we live at close quarters. Perfect mothers and perfect fathers do not exist—good ones perhaps, but not perfect ones.

And so we ask ourselves, how can a mother aim at living so that her children come to understand what human nature means? Certainly, a mother with this aim knows what discipline means. She knows discipline does *not* mean punishment.

I find that many mothers—and fathers, too—confuse discipline with punishment. But the two words don't mean the same thing at all. They come from entirely different roots. Discipline comes from the word from which we get "disciple"—someone who gives himself or herself to another person because he or she admires the person. A disciple admires the way a person speaks and behaves, and the way that person speaks and behaves disciplines the disciple. Discipline means women and men living in a way that attracts the respect and admiration of the younger people living with them.

As parents we have to decide whether we want to be educators or "angels with the flaming sword." And our decision will determine what disciplinary techniques we will use. The proud avenger of defined "rules and regulations" takes one kind of person; it takes another kind to guide a human being through the turmoil of growth. We have to make up our minds which we will be.

Undoubtedly, real discipline involves a particu-

lar kind of restraint. About as quick a way as any
to spot a mature Christian, if you happen to run
into one, is this: He or she accepts at least a share
of the blame when things go wrong—excuses are
not made.

But the inspired writer of Genesis apparently
understood our human tendencies very well. He
pictured the first man as putting the blame for his
wrongdoing on his wife, and Eve tried to shift the
blame to the snake. Jesus showed his understanding of human nature when he said, "They all with
one accord began to make excuses" (Luke 14:18,
NKJV). It seems to be a natural tendency for us,
like those of whom Paul wrote, to "establish their
own righteousness" rather than to accept the
righteousness of God (Rom. 10:3, NKJV).

As with most, I'm sure my own children reflect
with embarrassing accuracy this prevailing attitude that so often stands between me and Christian
integrity.

"Who did it?" I storm into their room demanding.

"It was Steve!" says Fay.

"It was Fay!" shouts Steve.

And even if I could find out who perpetrated the
crime, each would point to the other and insist,
"He made me do it." That may sound juvenile, but
so often I, too, try unsuccessfully to defend myself
even in the presence of God. In fact, sometimes life

seems all wrapped up in the "manly art of self-defense" as I blame everything that goes wrong on the administration or the multi-national corporations or the media. On the other hand, I find that in those moments when I admit that my troubles are at least in part my own fault, the door of God's grace seems to open for me.

Of course, we parents will have to correct and discipline our children. But we must be extremely careful about our own attitudes and make certain that our correction helps them and is not just a means of getting rid of our frustrations.

It is most important that we "keep our cool" as we strive to properly discipline and direct the lives of our children. Younger people need the confidence that only a steady hand and a settled soul can offer. A sensitive and "settled" mother can ladle out praise in generous portions to her children. This will not only raise their sense of self-worth but will enable them to accept her criticism and respect her judgment. Slowly, they can now begin to understand the meaning of human integrity as they have seen it modeled for them by a caring woman and man—their parents—who, although they recognize the natural tendency of children to live illogical, unreasonable, and self-centered lives, aim at loving and trusting them anyway. Such adults accept the fact that if you try to do good, people will accuse you of having selfish motives. But they aim at doing good anyway. They know that honesty and frankness leave a person wide open for criticism and hurt. But they aim at honesty and frankness anyway. They know that the biggest people with the biggest ideas can get shot down by the smallest people with the smallest minds. But they still aim at thinking big anyway. They know that what they spend years building may get destroyed overnight. But they aim at building anyway. They know that people who really need help may repel their efforts to help. But they aim at helping people anyway. They know that if you give the world the best you have, there is a possibility it won't be appreciated at all. But they aim at giving the world the best that they have anyway.

The caring woman and man will listen, instead of pretending to listen, to each other and to their children. How often we pretend to listen—maintain eyeball contact, nod, smile, and even answer occasionally—but behind the mask our minds are a thousand miles away. I "listen" to my son complain for the thirteenth time about his history prof, but I'm really thinking about the phone call I have to make. Or at times I listen selectively. I do that with television all the time to screen out commercials. But such selective listening creates problems when my wife or my children expect a thorough hearing. Topics of interest to them may at the time seem unimportant to me, so I tune out. It was only as I began to realize just how damaging my inattention and selective listening was to our relationship as a family that I began to work at keeping the lines of communication open.

Mozart's parents lived in a world of music. Both of them played instruments. They invited people to their home who enjoyed music and enjoyed making music and they surrounded their young son with an atmosphere of harmony and soaring melodies. Young Mozart was taken to concerts in the cathedrals and given the opportunity to express himself, to play, to write. They exposed him to the history and the mystery of the technique of music. In that sense they disciplined him and gave his spirit a chance to develop and to grow. Such an aim makes up for a host of mistakes along the way.

Of course, no mother or father can be certain beyond a doubt that their discipline and love won't be rejected. But that possibility must not inhibit our giving of love, for while we are assured that everything else may fail, love lasts—an uncalculating love for people, love for beauty, love for integrity, love for truth, love for justice, never ends.

A mother took her six-year-old boy into a doctor's crowded waiting room and as they waited their turn, he began to ask her all kinds of questions. In half an hour he managed to cover almost every subject known to humanity. To the wonder of all the others sitting in the room, his mother answered each query carefully and patiently. Inevitably he got around to God; and as the other people listened to his relentless "how's" and "why's," it was plain to see by the expressions on their faces that they wondered: "How does she stand it?"

But when she answered her son's next question, she answered theirs too.

"Why,"he asked, "doesn't God ever get tired and just stop?"

"Because," she replied after a moment's thought, "God is love; and love never gets tired."

There is so much about the time in which we are living that is confusing and complex. We are assaulted by constant change that staggers our imagination, but we can take into this new era a profound, uncalculating love for the people we live with and the world we live in.

As a person, I have plenty of things to work on and to discover. But I believe women and men can aim at keeping love for each other at full strength, particularly under stress, because it will cover innumerable times when our behavior will bring us short of our goals. And I believe such an atmosphere of love can seep out into our communities and find creative ways of making our world a better place in which to live.

I love to read James Thurber. Thurber stands

as one of the great humorists our country has produced. Almost blind himself, he had a way of seeing into life that brought out light and laughter and punched holes in pomposity. A year or two ago I read a biography Thurber wrote of Ross, his one-time boss and founder of the *New Yorker* magazine. Thurber noted that Ross sometimes threatened to quit the *New Yorker* and was at least twice threatened with being fired. But he kept on going like "a battle-torn flag and nobody captured his colors and nobody silenced his drums." I like that phrase. All around me I feel forces that threaten women and men either to drop out, to become angry, or to act irrationally. These forces are so powerful and complex that many of us do not understand them. They threaten to get the best of us. Precisely such a moment calls for a kind of woman and man that keeps on going "like a battle-torn flag and no one captures our colors and nobody silences our drums."

5

A

Little Child

Shall

Lead?

IN 1976 THE UNITED NATIONS GENERAL ASSEM-
bly designated 1979 as the International Year of
the Child. From the experts who toil with research
and statistics we learned that nearly 120 million
babies are born every year—more than three
every time my pulse throbs. Two-thirds of them
are born without the help of obstetrician or mid-
wife. We also learned that in some areas of the
world infant mortality runs as high as 40 percent.

These are mind-boggling statistics as we reflect
on the fact that such a large percentage of the
children make their entrance into the world under
precarious conditions. Much has been written

about the needs of children by experts who work with them. But put simply: children need protection, opportunity, and facilities to develop in a healthy and normal manner. They need freedom and dignity, love and understanding, and an atmosphere of affection and security. Above all, children need the care of responsible parents.

Responsible parenting has always been rather a tricky and hazardous occupation, and yet most people who marry, even today, express a desire to have children and build a family. In that process we all experience a lot of anxiety and pain, frequently because of our unreal expectations. Silly as it may seem, we expect children to act like adults and become outraged at their behavior when they are merely acting normal for their age. Often, too, we become so set in the rightness of our own ideas and our parent role that we just about have a nervous breakdown when a kid starts making sense in an argument. But with all the things said about what adults can do with and for children, I hear little about what children can do for adults. After all, we get the word education from Latin *erudire* which means "giving form to raw (rudis) material." In the Greek or Roman world education became the art of making out of the raw material of children responsible citizens, brave soldiers, or any other prominent adult educational ideal. For the ancient Semitic Hebrews, education meant to flog, discipline, or instruct. But both these societies, the Greco-Roman and the Jewish, saw children as objects of education. Mature adulthood was the goal.

At the same time I have come to believe there is a strong possibility that children have something important to say to adults. In spite of their childishness and immaturity their contribution to our lives can be most profound. After all, people thirty-six inches tall see the world differently than people seventy-two inches tall. They simply have a different point of view, and so often I have failed to see that both points of view may be valid. Unfortunately, I often tend to accept the seventy-two-inch point of view without question while ignoring or acting condescending to the three-footer because of his size or age. Somehow I had learned to think that because of size and age what a thirty-six-inch person sees is not valid. But slowly I have come to understand that a thirty-six-inch point of view may have validity.

Now I feel that if I had paid closer attention to children in the past I might have discovered things about myself I had missed. Children have a way of showing me who I am. I watch them play and see one act meanly and destroy the game for the others. Then I think of the games grown-up people play. A child can show me how much forgiveness I need. And suddenly I sense in children the mysterious presence of Christ. Jesus said, "Whoever receives one such child in my name, receives me; and whoever receives me, receives not me but him who sent me" (Mark 9:37, RSV; cf. Luke 9:48 and Matt. 18:5).

Many modern theologians have a great deal to say about whether or not we can see the presence of Christ among the poor of the world. But there is a strong tendency with most interpreters of the faith to ignore the truth that Christ moves and acts through children in ways that merit our close attention. Of course, I know the term "children" in these Scripture selections has a metaphorical meaning, standing for all "little ones," whether they are children or persecuted Christians, or even generally, all those who don't seem to count. But when Jesus said, "Whoever receives one such child in my name, receives me," he was certainly referring to actual children. So, in ways I cannot explain, Christ and the God who sent him seem present in ordinary children—playing or crying, tender or cruel, nicely washed or dirty.

I'm reminded here of the words of Jesus when he said, "Let the little children come to Me, and do not forbid them; for of such is the kingdom of God" (Luke 18:16, NKJV). What in the world does that mean? Slowly it dawns on me that the essence of the kingdom of God is the child locked up within me, age twenty-eight or thirty-eight or forty-eight or fifty-eight or ninety-eight. How does God get loose in the world? He's loose in the child growing up within you and me. And it was this same Jesus who, at another time, said something like this: "Except you grownups become converted and like a little child again, you will never see the kingdom of God." Imagine! The essence of life is the child in me that never stops growing unless I kill it. If the child-spirit in me dies, then no matter how long I live, my soul has lain down and died already.

What did Jesus mean by the child in me? I believe he meant that God let loose his creative essence in me, whether I ever married or had a child or not. Life takes on meaning as I let this childlike spirit of God within me emerge without choking, quenching, or abusing it.

Modern transactional analysis reminds me that I have a child locked inside of me—a child locked in by my grasping, covetous impulses. Something has to give. Somehow I have to let that locked-up child loose. And when I do, what refreshing changes that will bring. It is then the child within me awakens a sense of awe and wonder.

While visiting a young mother, a friend noticed that her four-year-old daughter kept interrupting her housework by coming in and insisting that her mother "come outside and see." She would then excitedly show her mother a flower or a butterfly or a broken bird's egg or a crawling caterpillar.

After this had happened for about the sixth time, the friend commented that these little trips sure interfered with the daily routine. "Well," replied the mother cheerfully, "I brought her into the world. The least I can do is let her show it to me."

Human spiritual development requires a sense of awe and wonder. Spirited people, like children, begin to see all of God's creation through new eyes. Yes, my children came from me. Yet they will always be beyond me. Their openness, their gentleness and spontaneity and capacity for love surprise me. And when I have had the sense to listen, I have heard them saying that I, too, had a childlike quality in me. Life means letting that spirit emerge without choking it.

The child in me knows no limit of hope. This child in me longs for a better life and the emergence of a glorious, godly style of living. I admit I often wound the child within me and imprison it. But it seems to keep coming to life again.

There have been times when I've caught myself wounding the child in my own children. I may not have slighted them, but I certainly criticized them—"You want the car too often." "Don't drive so fast." "You stay out too late." And I've heard parents say to children, "You're dumb" or "You're ugly" or "You're fat" or "You're thin" or you're this or that. How easy it is for us to apply labels. People grow up with the impression that life is one nagging criticism after the other.

Bryant Kirkland, while riding a Fifth Avenue bus in New York, noticed a squirmy little girl in a winter coat looking out of the window at the wonderful world passing by while her father busily read the newspaper. "Sit still, will you?" he grumbled. After a few minutes, "I said sit still," he shouted again.

Well, the child sat still. She may sit still for the rest of her life. Any child can tell a put down. But someday she may say, "I'm a person. There is something locked in me. I'm a human being. If I can't find it any other way, I'll smash my way out and find fulfillment."

There's an intriguing paradox loose in the world. It isn't so much that we "raise" children to act a certain way. Rather, children reproduce what we are. Showing a child how a happy adult lives does far more than trying to define mature behavior to a child. Do I want happy children? Suddenly, I have to ask myself, "Art, are you fun to live with?" I want creative children. But do I get excited about new ideas? I want them to learn. But how many books have I read in the last month, in the last year? I want them to have friends. Yet how friendly am I? I want them to have high ideals. But do I have any left, and are they important enough to show in what I do? Have I ever told my children what I deeply believe? I want them to be generous. How generous am I about the needs of anyone outside of my immediate family? In reflecting on these penetrating questions, I've concluded that while children may not treasure the things and ideas I want them to, they do value what we are.

Each generation needs the other. We need each other to mature and grow and develop the skills of life and love. Children teach us that. Watching them, I discover I can live alive in the present and at the same time be open to the future and expect the impossible. I can dare to challenge the hard facts of life today by the reality of a new day tomorrow. In this way, children have enlarged my world. They make me stretch my mind to answer searching questions, and they force me to broaden my social and political responsibilities for the health and welfare of children everywhere.

Children deepen my spiritual awareness. They confront me with my inadequacy as an adult. My children help me to learn how to love as well as seek love, and because of them I have to reorder my values according to new priorities. And when I think about it, I believe that simply by living with my children for awhile, I receive far more from them than I ever give them. God may love me as I am, but he loves me too much to leave me like I am.

Our children can reintroduce to us the wonders of the world we often take for granted. They can teach us a new sense of significance. I remember beginning to feel a new sense of importance because my children thought I was important. And because my children loved to create and learn and try new things, they lifted me out of old ruts and helped me to see the world with new eyes. Yes, I believe people can live in a larger, richer world if they allow children to lead them into it. As Oliver Wendell Holmes once commented, "Children do pretty much all of the honest truth-telling there is in the world."

6

Life

at

Close

Quarters

SHE HAD TWO PROBLEMS COMMON TO MANY STU-
dents: low grades and no money. How could she
explain it to mom and dad? After much thought she
took an inventive tack she hoped would prove productive. Erwin W. Lutzer in his book *Failure: The
Back Door to Success,** quotes her letter.

"Dear Mom and Dad,
    Just thought I'd drop you a note to clue you in on
my plans. I've fallen in love with a guy named Jim.
He quit high school after grade 11 to get married.
About a year ago he got a divorce.

---

*Published by Moody Press, © 1976.

We've been going steady for two months and plan to get married in the fall. Until then, I've decided to move into his apartment; I think I might be pregnant.

At any rate, I dropped out of school last week, although I'd like to finish college some time in the future."

On the next page she continued:

"Mom and dad, I just wanted you to know that everything I've written so far in this letter is false. None of it is true. But it is true that I got a C— in French and flunked Math. It IS true that I am going to need some more money for my tuition payments."

Sharp girl!

Life at close quarters often calls for fast footwork. Without it, reason totters, imagination reels, and humor loses its balance. And that kind of stress gives us plenty of opportunity to feel pain.

Dr. Hans Selye, perhaps the world's foremost authority on stress, believes that practically all human diseases have their origin in stress. I know from experience that the stress of living at close quarters can often affect my allergies and sometimes my lower back.

But the girl who wrote this letter discovered that she could make bad news look like good news from a certain vantage point—it was a matter of per-

spective. This reminds me that I need to get perspective on life at close quarters. I need to develop
a way of distinguishing between the incidental and
the essential—the temporary and the eternal, the
partial and the whole, the trees and the forest.

We all arrived on this planet without any advance preparation. But it didn't take us long to
learn that things seldom go according to plan. A
single adjective describes almost every future
event: unexpected. Unexpected illness . . . unexpected transfer . . . unexpected accomplish-
ment . . . unexpected surgery, promotion, gift,
death.

Everybody makes plans. When the University
of Southern California and Ohio State University
played in the Rose Bowl on New Year's Day, 1980,
both teams made plans. They diagrammed plays
and spent hours working on the execution of those
plays. After practice they studied movies of the
opposing team. They even narrowed down their
study to the style of individual players. And all of
this preparation led to the development of a game
plan for each team.

Yet, with all the planning, we have to leave room
for the unexpected. The wind shifts or the ball
takes an unexpected bounce and suddenly we have
to improvise. We take chances we hadn't planned
on. We find ourselves living by faith.

And that's not so easy when the Bible doesn't

cover every problem we have to face. It doesn't, you know. The Bible leaves whole areas unaddressed. Many times I can't find an explicit answer in the Bible for my particular problem. At just such times I have to live by faith. I have to trust God to show me the next step to take. The Bible simply does not give a specific answer to every problem in life.

Well, then, what about the stress that living with people at close quarters brings today? I doubt if anyone who is looking for a blueprint for all of life will ever make much progress. And, yet, we have to plan as best we can. My wife and I made plans for the birth of our first child. We read all the books we could get our hands on. During those blissful childless days we observed mistakes others made in rearing children. Then all at once we found ourselves living at close quarters with a real baby. He brought with him changes we had not planned on. Living at close quarters helps me see that what happens *in* me can cause far more stress than what happens *to* me.

The stress is not in my circumstances. The stress is in me. I decide in my head what kind of stress any circumstance will give me. I put my own meaning into events. Some people fly in airplanes for sheer joy. Other people avoid flying at all cost. The same airplane will produce delight in some and distress in others.

Now I see that stress has two faces. Some stress does me a lot of good, as when my heart pounds for joy when I see my daughter for the first time in months. But other stress tears me up. We each put our own meaning into events.

A few years ago cartoonist Jules Feiffer pictured a woman thinking these thoughts to herself: "I used to wonder how I'd stand up to the worst moment in my life. I stood up to the Depression but I didn't think it was the worst moment in my life. I stood up to my parents' death, but I didn't think it was the worst moment in my life. I stood up to my husband cheating on me, but I didn't think it was the worst moment in my life. I stood up to my children deserting me, but I didn't think it was the worst moment in my life. The worst moment in my life is when I realized: This is my life. I don't know if I can stand up to it."

Of course what happens to me does affect me. Sometimes something hits me out of the blue and stops me in my tracks and turns me around in a completely new direction. It feels like the time my father tumbled me out of his lap. In college days I enjoyed playing the piano. To improve what little talent I had I used to listen to the piano artistry of Art Tatum. I still have a collection of a number of his records. I remember when he resurrected an old tune from the 1920s which went "I Guess I'll Have to Change My Plan." A phrase in the song goes, "Before I knew where I was at I found myself upon the shelf and that was that." Living at close quarters has a way of doing that to me when I've made other plans. A man suddenly finds himself unemployed. He hadn't planned on that. His plans for the future evaporate like the morning dew. That's bad enough. But plenty of people who have a job feel unemployed at the point of living itself. They work hard enough, but inside they wonder if all this effort, all this energy, all this time mean anything? Does it mean anything to me? Will it produce anything that will last?

And this feeling can spill over into a marriage relationship. My wife and I sat at dinner with some friends. One woman at the table told of a friend of hers who had begun to wear several rings on her left hand, but she wore her wedding ring on the index finger. She couldn't help asking, "Betty, aren't you wearing your wedding ring on the wrong finger?"

"You bet!" she said, "I married the wrong man."

But back to planning—I'm the kind of person who likes to look before he leaps. I buy life insurance, plan vacations a year in advance, and I get my teeth checked once or twice a year. I carefully examine references before hiring. And if I'm going to make a major purchase, I may consult *Consumer Research*. Who can deny the virtue of any of that? Yet sometimes all this planning leads to an emotional overload. Here's a man earning between $18,000 and $30,000 a year. He feels suspended just above poverty and far below affluence. Rising prices erode his salary every year. Credit payments for the car, the house, keep him scrambling. He has a close friend, a little older, a child of the Depression who went through World War II and on to college on the G.I. Bill. But his friend has to run hard just to keep up because the promotions and invitations he longed for now go to people ten to fifteen years his junior. These two men fiercely want to live life out, not just wobble through it somehow. And so colleges now offer courses in assertiveness training to show us how we can make it by standing up for our personal rights. Such courses often emphasize how we can win even though someone else must lose. They tell us how to get more even though someone else will have to do with less.

Yet it is no simple matter. Neither is life. I can always find an Einstein or an Albert Schweitzer, or a Bach, or someone who made a million dollars in real estate to compare myself to. Such comparisons fill us with terrible stress. Why do we make such unrealistic demands on ourselves? Probably to compensate for some deeply felt inner inadequacy. And I see all kinds of people do it to themselves. They remind me of the woman who went into a very fashionable apartment house, got into the elevator, and asked the operator to take her to the eleventh floor. As they started up, he said, "Ma'am, who is it you want to see on the eleventh floor?"

"It is none of your business," she said.

"Ma'am, I'm not trying to pry, but this building only has eight floors."

So sometimes in my planning I put myself under all kinds of stress because I set an unrealistic goal for myself. Besides, I sometimes get too tense about living at close quarters. I worry about stress doing some permanent damage to my mind or my emotions or my body. But the facts don't bear out such worries. Normal stress can bless my human nature. It can actually add spice to my life. Without some stress, most of us would never solve many of our problems. Activity involves stress. To exercise means stressing my muscles. Without it the world's work would never get done. Life is a bit like a violin string. It needs enough tension to make music, but not so tight that it will snap. And it shouldn't hang so loose that it is dull and toneless. We need just the right balance of tension. In this sense stress remains essential to life. We'd die without it.

My problem is not with feeling stress but rather with an overload which gives me pain. It isn't severe enough to be pathological stress. Rather, it is the ordinary overload that many of us face far too often. What good will it do us if we build a magnificent civilization and lose emotional control of our lives?

I don't know why some things cause me more stress than others, or why such events don't affect other people the same way. But I know I must discover some way to cope with life at close quarters.

Victor Frankl likes to quote Frederick Nietzsche: "He who knows the *why* to his existence can endure any *how*." I need to wrestle with the why of my existence. As important as the question, "Who am I?" is the resounding counter question of "Where am I going?" Do the plans I make have anything to do with an overall direction in life? My stomach turns over and my neck begins to cramp up when I'm not sure what I'm doing is the right thing. Or when I'm not sure what to do next. Or when I'm not sure what priority to give things. If I feel confident about the direction in which I'm living, it helps take the pain out of the stress involved in moving in that direction.

Engstrom and Dayton, in their book *Strategy for Living,* helped bring finding direction into focus. They suggest that we imagine what kind of life we want to live and where we want to live it ten to fifteen years from today. Then we can let that image help us establish our long-range purposes.

And in the light of that we can sort out what we want to do and those things we don't want to do.

The next step is to move back from that future date to a closer time. What should we do and where should we be three years from now? Then with these in mind move back to one year from now. Now we find ourselves dealing with very specific things. We can sort them out and note the ones we have responsibility for. If we know the direction we should be going this year, it gives us the context in which to know what we should be doing this month. And knowing that will help clarify what we will do tomorrow morning.

This exercise helps me accept myself as I am. Even so, it isn't easy living at close quarters in our society. The pressure is continually on me to become someone else, either more handsome or the owner of a prestige automobile. Advertising works on the principle of making me dissatisfied with myself.

A man was heard to say, "I feel pulled in a hundred directions. I hardly know who I am. I am a husband. I am a father. I am a salesman. I am an employee. I belong to a veterans' group. I am a good American. I am a good guy. I am each of these things. And each of them tries to tell me what to do. I feel pulled in a hundred directions. Besides, I'm a part-time Christian. I say part-time because most of the time I have trouble living out my faith.

I can live it part of the time, when those things seem real and important to me. But the rest of the time I don't feel like I am a Christian in any sense that matters much to God at all."

I know the feeling. Christian sometimes. Not so Christian on the golf course. Less than Christian in some areas. Definitely suspect in quite a few others. Sometimes I'm patient and understanding with a "crashing bore" who strains my patience to the limit. And then I'm short-tempered with someone who really deserves my patience and love.

Besides, the expectations people have of me often give me an anxiety attack. I know I don't live up to their expectations for me. And their expectations often simply confirm my doubts about myself. A man left church one Sunday saying, "Reverend, I loved your sermon. It was just like water to a drowning man!" I know I often don't live up to people's expectations, no matter how real or unreal those expectations are. Worse yet, I often don't live up to my own expectations. I'm not perfect. I don't know anyone who is. I don't do everything well. But I do do some things well.

I believe we can begin to come to terms with stress by accepting ourselves as we are at our age. We can look forward to good things yet to come rather than regretting what might have been. So often we carry an unflattering picture of ourselves around in our heads, and we don't like what we see. At least, I have had that experience. But I need to rip up that grotesque caricature that fills me with such low self-esteem. I need to see myself as somebody. I don't need to compare myself with anybody else. There's no one like me. Then I begin to develop a new picture of myself in my mind.

What we think affects who we are. If we keep saying, "I'm not good. I can't do it," we put all kinds of stress on our bodies. We just have to tear up that old picture and throw it away. But to do that requires learning how to develop an inner stillness that goes beyond what psychologists and psychotherapists often talk about. The inner stillness I'm talking about has to do with spirit rather than feelings.

My ability to cope with stress depends upon my spiritual interior. If I have a divided loyalty there between what society tells me to do and what I believe I should do, I am constantly torn back and forth. So I have to put values on those pressures. I can cope with stress by seeing it as part of life and by putting proper value on it.

In the stillness I come to know I am not created by other people. I am not judged by how I compare with others. If I can get up in the morning believing I am not a stranger simply blundering through a blind universe, but a friend of a living God; if I know each day that one unending purpose runs through all life and I am not at the mercy of forces that beat me down but am held by a power nothing can defeat—then the horizon of life will look brighter and new power will surge through my life.

An old song in the Bible runs, "Don't be worried on account of the wicked; don't be jealous of those who do wrong. They will soon disappear like grass that dries up; they will die like plants that wither. Trust in the Lord and do good; live in the land and be safe. Seek your happiness in the Lord, and he will give you your heart's desire. Be patient and wait for the Lord to act; don't be worried about those who prosper or those who succeed in their evil plans. Don't give in to worry or anger; it only leads to trouble" (Ps. 37:1–4, 7, 8 TEV).

So, in the secret citadel of my soul I have begun to discover that God is on the spot when I am in a bind. The word "trouble" in Hebrew means "squeezed into a narrow, cramped place." That describes how I feel when stress is doing a number on me. Precisely when I am hard-pressed, I can expect to find God in the pressure of that moment.

But entering into such inner stillness is not as easy as it sounds. I tend to overschedule myself. Rarely do I finish an hour's work in an hour. There are too many interruptions. Furthermore, I sometimes don't know when to quit. Animals do. Animals retreat from a losing battle. But super-competitive humans like me don't quit, and we make ourselves suffer as a result. Stress becomes pain when we do too much of the same thing for too long. To create some sense of inner quiet we have to ask ourselves if what confronts us is worth fighting for. Does changing this person's opinion or correcting this situation really make any difference in the course of world events?

My wife tells how her fourth-grade teacher returned from a trip to Egypt to inspire her class with exotic tales of the pyramids. She never forgot those stories. So a year ago off we went on a trip that took us from Athens to Cairo to Israel. For over two weeks I didn't see a newspaper or TV newscast. And, you know, when I got home it didn't matter one iota! I found people saying the same old things they'd said before. I wondered why I had let them tense me up so before we left.

Furthermore, I find that trying to simplify helps ease my stress. I can strive for excellence in a few things. I find I can cut down on trying to accumulate things in a time of inflation and reduce the stress-filled burden of paying for them. That leaves me time to use my limited abilities creatively. I have time to pay attention to what happens here and now right under my nose. I don't have to travel all over the world to see the beauty of creation. I can discover it in one flower.

Slowly it dawns on me that living successfully at close quarters is not so much a matter of what happens to me, or what I have to do, as it is who I am. If I think of life as something I have—a sort of possession—I always set myself up for disappointment. Of course, I tend to identify myself by what I have (houses, cars, boats) and do (my job, my achievements, vita sheets), but, in reality, life at close quarters comes down to a matter of being.

Carlyle Marney once told of a young teenage woman paraplegic, without hands or legs, a strong voice, or mobility. An insensitive social worker asked if she wouldn't as soon end it all. The girl cheerfully replied, "I wouldn't have missed being for anything." How slowly it dawns on me that I have worth, not because of what I have or what I do, but because all life—your life, even my life— has significance now.

Mary Craig had four sons. One boy has an honors degree and works in a large computer organization. One will get his doctorate in psychology. But she has two younger boys. One is a mongoloid. "Not a very bad case," said the doctor at his birth. At thirteen he stood tall and apparently strong, but remained a baby with a baby's need for protection. Yet he is a happy boy, the focal point of the family. He is a television fanatic. He knows the commercials by heart, and he knows which button to press if the color goes wrong.

"Nicky never stops producing joy and love wherever he goes," wrote a journalist. Nicky was the fourth baby. But there was a second younger son—Paul. He always seemed hungry as a baby and always cried. "In retrospect," said Mary Craig, "it seems to me he didn't stop crying for the first five years, but I suppose memory is playing me false. He *must* have slept sometimes." At two Paul went to the hospital with a strangulating hernia. The doctor in the emergency room had come from a Mideastern country and had no more than a sketchy idea of English. "You're the mother of . . . er . . . er . . ." He riffled through the papers in his hand. "Ah, yes, Paul Craig?" Mary Craig nodded. "Of course you know he's not normal?" She stared at him blankly. Her world slowly dissolved as reality crystalized in that one murderous phrase, "not normal." "He has Höhler's Syndrome, a rare disease. In English you call it . . . er . . . gargoylism." Mary Craig and her husband kept Paul at home and faced the stress and pain inflicted thoughtlessly by others. A woman on a bus said, "Children like that shouldn't be allowed in public. It's not right."

A doctor and family friend almost shouted, "An animal, that's what he is, an animal. Why don't you have him put away?"

Paul went to countless clinics so that specialists could look at this interesting case of a rare disease and talk about it to bored students as they poked and prodded Paul, pointing out his symptoms.

Small wonder Mary almost broke under the

strain. One evening she found herself in an empty church. "I didn't howl, but muttered, defiant if muddled, 'Damn you, you don't exist, but I hate you.' Then I burst into tears and threw decorum to the wind. 'All right,' I heard myself shouting, 'if you do exist, show me a way out. For a start, what in blazes am I to do next?' After this unbridled exhibition I was startled by the noise I was making and ran out of the church at top speed."

The way out came by way of an advertisement for helpers at Sue Ryder's Home for concentration-camp survivors and led across Europe to Poland. There among people who had been starved, beaten, tortured, and experimented upon, Mary found spontaneous joy and faith.

"The value of suffering," Mary writes, "does not lie in the pain . . . but what the sufferer makes of it . . . the real tragedy in suffering is the wasted opportunity."

I have a feeling that to live at close quarters means to face all that makes us miserable and ashamed, and to continue to press for the love that lies beneath the agony.

"They that wait upon the Lord shall renew their strength:
They shall mount up with wings as eagles;
They shall run and not be weary;
And they shall walk and not faint."

7

Back

to

Work

Again?

I REMEMBER THE MORNING MILLIE LEFT FOR work. We became a two-paycheck family again. Nor did she just go out to get a job. Starting in the field of cancer research, she soon found herself in management as administrator of the Division of Medical Oncology for the Department of Internal Medicine at the University of Southern California County Medical Center. Slowly I realized we had become not simply a two-paycheck family, but a two-career family. Suddenly, brand-new questions began to bubble up inside of me. How would her career affect my career mobility and vice versa? Those who refuse to move seldom get another chance. Who moves to San Francisco when one partner is offered the job of his or her dreams there? Suppose her career begins to rise as mine begins to set? What will happen to our relationship when she brings home more money than I do?

Meanwhile—back at home—who will wash the dishes?

Who will call the plumber when the pipes explode?

Who pays the bills and with whose money?

Suddenly, I see one of the big issues in a two-career marriage. Who has responsibility for the household? When Millie went back to work it took us three or four years to sort this out. We found that many old ideas did not fit our new situation.

Now, you can love someone. You can respect him. But there are still dinner dishes to do. And we have social obligations to arrange. Whose boss comes to dinner on which night? Whose company Christmas party takes priority? How shall we coordinate vacations?

The point is that in a two-career marriage the relationship often gets what's left over.

And what about sex?

Who has time?

Women have a tough time making their way in a man's world. After all, they have to deal with men—mates as well as employers. At work we talk about a businessman as aggressive, but a businesswoman is pushy. He loses his temper because he is involved with his job. She's a witch. He's a man of the world. She's been around. He's confident. She's conceited. He's a stern taskmaster. She's impossible to work for. Women fight an uphill battle to overcome these images so long a part of our cultural heritage. Besides, our heritage taught generations of women to fall in love, marry, and stay at home to raise a family. Young women have a hard time declaring their independence of a lifestyle their parents would have them live. But in spite of legitimate concern for home, well over 50 percent of married women in the United States work. The biggest jump occurred in the 1960s and '70s. In 1940 only 17 percent of all married women worked for wages. In 1974 the figure climbed to 43 percent. It now approaches 60 percent. Many of these women do not work because they feel a need of liberation or self-fulfillment. Most of them work because they have to. Families nowadays simply need both incomes. Yet working often gives a woman a new sense of identity. She is no longer just someone's wife. And she resents the accusation that she has run away from children for a glamorous career downtown.

In 1976 Alan Greenspan, economic advisor to President Ford, told reporters he had no idea why so many women had taken it into their heads to go to work, but he didn't think it had anything to do with the high cost of living. However, the flood of women going back to work continued in 1977. In fact, in her book, *The Two Paycheck Marriage*, Caroline Bird contends that working women were the ace-in-the-hole that saved the economy in the 1970s from the ravages unemployment had created during the Depression of the 1930s. About half of the unemployed husbands in the country had wives who were earning a paycheck. Their earnings kept health insurance policies in force and prevented the wholesale repossession of goods bought on credit, which had long worried fiscal conservatives.

Working wives help families maintain their standards of living through inflation. The Bureau of Labor Statistics has calculated that between 1973 and 1974 real purchasing power of single-earner families dropped 3 percent compared with only 1 percent with families in which the wife worked. The experts and the people themselves said it again and again: "With high prices it takes two to earn." Women will especially put themselves out to defend the standard of living they see threatened.

Working wives lifted millions of families into middle-class life. Her pay meant the difference between an apartment and a house, or college for the children.

For a couple to handle two careers they must

become outstandingly good managers. They have to sort out schedules, pay for transportation and child care, and muddle through the psycho-logistics of watering their marriage garden while alternating toiling at the office. I've even noticed that many thoughtful leaders of the women's movement have begun to do some fresh thinking.

Women often try to take all the old wifely values to work with them. Some try to play the role of "superwoman"—super mother, super wife, super lover, super worker. No wonder more than a few women feel burned out, used up, angry, and cynical. Many are high achievers. Because of that, they feel they aren't achieving enough.

So what can she do? First, be aware of it. Women often deny what's happening and even work harder. Soon she has a cold that doesn't go away or recurring headaches or finds herself dependent on valium or alcohol.

Ann Berk, station manager of WRC-TV, wrote in the September 29, 1980, issue of *Newsweek*, "Most working women in their thirties and forties are physically exhausted and emotionally drained, hysteria nibbling around the edge of their lives. They're the ones that still believe in having babies, who were taught to please men and sometimes even enjoy it. And while they no longer worry about floors you can eat off of, they find it hard to shelve their children's needs and desires, however quaint in 1980, or their men. Those in their twenties who think they have a lock on sanity because they have decided against having children and permanent attachments may wake up when they are fifty, if they haven't succumbed to a heart attack or lung cancer, to find themselves curiously empty.

"Women's magazines, those helpful guides through the morass, used to be filled with articles on how to be virginal after marriage, how to turn hamburger into filet mignon, how to bake cookies that smile, now tell us how to write a resume, how to dress for work, how to decorate our offices, how to be assertive, how to cope. Words. Reams and reams of words so precise and well-meaning and useless when it's 8:25 A.M. and your child can't find a clean shirt or the math book she left at a friend's house and the sitter didn't show and you are late for a meeting with a client and the dog is under the bed and refuses to go out for a walk— and at 8:00 P.M. when the guests you invited to dinner are waiting on the doorstep when you arrive, panting, having just left a crisis at the office to find the pasta place closed and your menu down the drain, and dog poop on the rug greeting you as you enter. The theories are nice. The realities are Erma Bombeck nightmares."

And so today many thoughtful women recognize that a kind of feminine machoism has seduced them. A machoism that confuses hostility with power. They made the same mistake as the male machos. Of course there is a difference between men and women. But I have to remember there is a difference between all people. Among men, I see passive and aggressive persons. And introspective persons. And outgoing persons. And persons oriented to tasks and others towards relationships. And I have a feeling that the spectrum of difference among working men is much broader than the general difference between men and women in working situations. But some women found themselves giving up feminine characteristics and taking on the worst characteristics of the male—for instance, toughness. At first glance it looks like the flinty, tough boss gets work done right away. But over the long haul his productivity goes down and down and down. Why? Because people don't like to work for him. They quit, or when he takes a vacation they goof off.

And then add to this confusion of hostility and power the fact that many women grew up not feeling good about themselves. They walk by a mirror and see all the things wrong with their hair or their face or their figure or their weight. At a deeper level they somehow succumb to the idea that teaching two children at home was somehow worse than teaching forty children of other people in school and getting paid for it. A confusion in the understanding of independence developed.

Can a two-career family or a single-parent family be a perfectly good family? Why not? The marvelous bonds of love and care that get adults hooked on each other and on a child—and a child on an adult—remain strong in many new kinds of families.

Too often adults ask themselves what they're doing wrong and not how forces of society pressure them. Society has not caught up with the two-career marriage. The phone company still won't tell me when they're going to send someone to fix the phone. They figure the wife will be there to take care of things. We try to change the victims of our society rather than change the forces that victimize.

Yet two people living and working at close quarters can begin with themselves. We can only bring to each other what we are. And a greater part of who I am I achieve through work. Still, two people can bet their lives on work that means something to both of them. That's quite different than simply working for financial security. It gives people a chance to find security *and* happiness. At least they will do what they want to do.

Today a man and woman who both work can contribute toward mutual goals. My wife helped support me through graduate school. Later I supported her through the childbearing years. Later still, when our children lived more outside the home than in it, Millie launched out into a career of her own.

My wife frankly prefers personnel management and administration to gourmet cooking and cleaning bathrooms. When Millie went to work I discovered that what was good for her as an individual was also good for our relationship.

I believe a woman needs satisfying and productive work just as a man does. Many women find that in the traditional occupations in the home. But today picture a bright young girl freshly married, moving into a tiny apartment or condominium. She quickly discovers that our technological society can produce almost everything cheaper outside the home than she can in it. Her cramped living quarters offer few challenges for her energy.

I know some men dread the fact that their wives may bring home larger salaries than they do. That can easily happen in the first years of marriage. A good secretary will earn more than a young doctor. At this point a young man and woman can strengthen their relationship if they talk about "our" instead of "mine" and "yours." It's not a case of "I earn so much and you earn so much." But rather "we" earn this income whether the paycheck has his or her name on it.

Working men and women live lives full of stress and strain. A current rise in the divorce rate seems connected to the fact that working women come in

contact with men more attractive and interesting
than their husbands. Fifty percent of divorces are
work-related. Either the man or woman met someone more interesting at work.

Anyone loose in the abrasive world of savage,
competitive business knows the extraordinary toll
in terms of emotional exhaustion. If both people
work, who will have the energy for the art and
effort of emotional and physical and spiritual re-
newal? God knows they both need it. Working couples cannot bypass this need for long without
paying the price of a serious depletion.

I do believe people can discover creative ways of
bringing physical and spiritual healing to each
other. Without feeling at all guilty, Millie and I
employ someone to clean the house on a regular
basis. We use the laundromat as much as the wash-
ing machine. Each month we take turns planning a
celebrative event. Something really special. Not
just another night out for dinner at a fast food
place.

We try to take care of our bodies. Millie enjoys
aerobic dancing and I maintain a daily thirty-min-
ute fitness program.

Early on we learned to laugh at ourselves. Try
it. It helps a lot.

And we spend an hour or so each evening just
talking through what happened to us that day at
work. She tells me about the foibles of people I've

never met. As she does, my world expands. We don't set a time to do this. It just sort of happens. I sometimes feel a little tongue-tied because I'm afraid telling her about my day would bore her limp. But knowing I have someone who's interested in hearing about it keeps me alert to what's happening in other people's lives around me as well as my own. Sometimes she'll ask for advice, which I'm always eager to give out of my more than adequate store!

Yet such seemingly surface chatter has a way of allowing deep spiritual needs and common values to surface.

But nothing brings deep healing to me more than hearing my wife say, "Art, you're doing a great job." Just to know she believes in my competence is one of the greatest renewers of energy in the world for me. So I let her know I believe in the importance of her career and in her competence. Such faith in each other renews life and hope.

Work itself has deep spiritual meaning. I believe in an active not a lazy God. When Moses heard a voice from a burning bush ordering him to lead the Israelites out of Egypt, he asked for the name of him who gave the command. The answer came in a riddle: "I am who I am." Ancient Hebrew had two tenses, the imperfect and the perfect. The fact that this answer is in the imperfect— a form denoting lack of completion—has implications for me. It seems to characterize the God of Moses as unceasing in his efforts. To me that equates the essence of life with activity.

And yet, as Mike Royko once noted in the *Chicago Daily News,* "If we asked people on the assembly lines, the punch presses, the open hearths, the loading platforms, the stock rooms, the freight elevators, the mail rooms, the boiler rooms, how their morale is, most would say: 'Are you crazy?' "

Try stopping off at a coffee shop, where the salesmen are getting together with their district manager before going off to peddle a product they don't care about, and ask why their stomachs are knotted. Salesmen have to give themselves pep talks about positive thinking. If they don't, they might head for a bar instead of a customer.

Get on a commuter train and see how many beaming, smiling faces there are as they approach another shift of making the rent. It's not the weather that gives them that weary look so early in the day.

And these are people with jobs. For a real look at low morale, try the waiting rooms of the employment agencies, or talk with some of the men who are cut from skilled jobs after they turn forty.

A friend of mine on a week's visit to Iona Community in Scotland learned that the founder and leader of that community, the Reverend Sir George Macleod, undertook the cleaning out of the toilets during the community work period. When someone asked Dr. Macleod why he chose such an undesirable task, he retorted, "It's to prevent me from preaching sermons on the dignity of work."

Here's a report of a sociologist's interview in an American factory:

"What do you do?"

"I make C-28."

"What is C-28?"

"I don't know."

"How long have you been working here?"

"Ten years."

Now, we might eulogize the village blacksmith, but how do you eulogize the fabricator of C-28? Does a modern carpenter beat his chest and say, "I'm building a warehouse to store cosmetics, wines, and beer"?

Yet not all work is trivial, useless, or immoral. I believe we still live in God's world. Adam started working before he started sinning. A person who works is happier than a person who is idle.

Of course, Luther went on to say that a dairymaid "milked cows to the glory of God." We have only the preacher's word for it, not the dairymaid's. Dairy conditions have changed today. I don't mean people can't glorify God in a dairy, but I do think we often make the issue too simple when it's not. A lot of romantic nonsense gets tossed out from church pulpits about the joy and delight of honest toil. There's talk about work as constant satisfaction and a great opportunity to serve God and humanity. I've seen depressed men and women leave church wondering how that picture matches the daily work that awaits them in the office, the store, or the kitchen sink.

Of course, some people find their jobs satisfying. Yet every job involves a lot of sheer drudgery. Jesus, with his constant talk about daily work—in the home, the field, the marketplace—clearly knew the basic importance of drudgery and never tried to disguise it as a constant source of joy and excitement.

We all depend on a huge amount of sheer drudgery on the farms, in factories, and in transportation to keep us alive. Plowing fields, digging wells, driving trucks, working on assembly lines—without such drudgery I couldn't have eaten breakfast this morning or had any clothes to wear.

The realistic Bible I read doesn't allow any room for the idea that somehow faith in God offers an escape from the drudgery of work. Of course, there is no Christian virtue in the acceptance of unnecessary drudgery and monotony, but it's an illusion to think that the life of my mind and spirit, the setting of new insights, the creation of truth, goodness, and beauty is somehow an escape from sheer hard work. Sheer drudgery lies behind the production of the most brilliant masterpiece of art just as it does behind the easy patter of a skilled comedian or the apparently effortless grace of a golf champion.

Paderewski was one of the greatest pianists in the world, and one of the hardest practicers in the world. He thought nothing of playing a bar or phrase of music forty or fifty times before a performance to get it just right. He once played before Queen Victoria.

"Mr. Paderewski," she said, "you're a genius."

"That may be," answered Paderewski, "but before I was a genius I was a drudge."

I do not believe that any great thing was ever done easily. I believe in activity and work. It seems a fact that only dedicated drudgery can give people satisfaction of mind and spirit. So, work remains important in society, more important than many technologists realize.

Yet, it's not all there is to life. Allen Richardson has tried to rescue the word "vocation" from the clutch of "vocational guidance instructors." When I read the Bible, I suddenly see that vocation and what I do for a living are not the same thing. I can't find God calling anyone in the New Testament to the particular job by which they earned their living. Paul was not "called" by God to be a tentmaker but to be an apostle.

Yes, a job well done is a service rendered to God, but the "vocation" is essentially the same to everyone: a calling to repent, have faith, and to serve Christ. The way I earn my living is not an end in itself, but a means to the service of God.

What a liberating concept. What healing it brings at a time when the world of work has turned sour for so many and when so many of us define ourselves by what we do—"salesman," "contractor," "secretary," "housewife," "unemployed."

Essentially, I am a person called to an active Christian life. That's my vocation. That's who I am. Incidentally, I am a preacher. That's my avocation. How I earn my living. One may serve the other, but they are not the same.

Now, I believe this has implications for me personally and for the fabric of our society. During the first two centuries of American life, hard work—indeed all activity—took its primary value not from what it did for the individual but from what it contributed to the glory of God and the welfare of the community. The public interest took first place in the early American scale of values.

America was founded on the idealism of people who felt an enormous responsibility to their Lord and to their fellows. They worked with immense energy. And they saw work as a good thing so long as the gains were not misspent on luxuries. They seemed to feel that ultimately the gains of work were less important than the activity itself—an effort on behalf of a wider interest than the individual's own. Inspired by such values and blessed with abundant resources, they made the American wilderness flower.

Even Benjamin Franklin, long thought an exponent of hard work only if it were in the interest of the individual, insisted that work be viewed as good for the individual only if it contributed to the well-being of society. Which reminds me that "God so loved the world. . ."

8

The

Lift

of

Friendship

WHAT MAKES YOU OR ME DIFFERENT FROM A BA-
boon? Friendship! Dr. Richard Leakey continues
the research of his famous parents into the dawn of
human history. In his book *People of the Lake* he
describes explorations in Northern Kenya.

Now I don't want to get into any debate about
creation. But those old bones speak. Leakey says
that what separated human beings from the
chimps and baboons was not so much their intelligence as their generosity. It was sharing, not
hunting or gathering as such, that enhanced our
human qualities.

Here's an anthropologist, not a psychologist or a

philosopher, saying friendship humanizes creation. No one can teach or measure friendship. Yet isolation breeds so much emotional pain.

Many friendships dart over the surface of life like longlegged water bugs. The checker at the grocery store says, "Have a good day," as she hands me my change. We have little in common. Like stars in the solar system we move in our own orbits. Yet we have a friendship of convenience. We greet each other as we pass in the cosmic night.

A recent television series, "Danger UXB," reminded me of how duchesses and chimney sweeps drank tea together in deep air-raid shelters during World War II, when the danger of bombs made social distinction stupid. But mercifully the war ended. Unfortunately, so did many wartime friendships. *Punch* carried a cartoon of a man looking up from his paper in a railroad compartment and saying, "You need not be so matey; the war is over now."

A top New York executive had just come down to breakfast when the maid announced a Mr. George Johnson was at the door to see him. "By all means, bring him in," he said. When Mr. Johnson stepped in, the host greeted him warmly and recalled the wonderful visit he and his family had had at the beautiful Johnson ranch out West.

He remembered his children on horseback and the wonderful rides over the plains. What beautiful parties and dinners Mrs. Johnson had arranged. "My friend," concluded this eastern executive, "I hope you'll allow me the privilege of returning at least some of the great hospitality you showed to us."

Mr. Johnson sat somewhat subdued while the other man recalled those enjoyable times. Noticing his silence, his host pressed him for an explanation.

Finally Johnson told of the death of his wife when fire demolished their ranch home. Recovering from the shock of that statement our eastern friend noted that of course Johnson still had his wide-ranging business interest to keep his mind busy during such a period of grief.

"No," said Johnson, "after the fire everything just seemed to fall apart." Several businesses collapsed, one of his children fell hopelessly ill, the other boy spaced out on drugs, and Johnson himself spent several months in a hospital with . . .

"James, James," shouted the eastern executive in an anguished voice, "throw this man out—the stupid jerk is breaking my heart."

So many human friendships simply skim along the surface of life. But people get lonely when they do not take time to develop friendship at a deeper level. From the moment of conception friendship, like childbirth, takes time. Yet, paradoxically, an excessive desire to have friends creates an atmosphere of loneliness inside of me. The more I look for friends, the less I have. The less friends I have, the less friendly I become. And the less friendly I become, the less able I am to befriend anyone else.

Here's a man who constantly demands attention from his wife, saying that she doesn't appreciate him. So she began to watch the football games he loved and she loathed. But she also began to begrudge the time she gave to him. People have to give friendship freely. When people demand it, they kill it.

Sometimes friendship means simply backing off. I need to relax my intensity and refuse to force an issue. If the fish aren't biting, it doesn't do any good to beat the water with an oar.

"At the heart of love," some unknown preacher wrote, "there is a simple secret: the lover lets the beloved be free."

"Love is not possessive," Paul wrote in his famous chapter on love. Friendship requires a little slack in the rope sometimes. That's a hard pill for a parent like me to swallow. I get impatient and rigid and unbending and rush foolishly in where angels loathe to tread. And the result? Exasperated kids, rooms choked with threats, and irritating pressure. Living at close quarters requires some free space in relationships.

Sometimes a hard-selling salesman presses me to buy when I am trying to make up my mind. The faster he talks, the harder he pushes, the less interested I become—even if I want and need the article. A wise salesman knows when to give me the privilege of deciding for myself. He simply backs off and leaves me alone.

The president of an insurance company called on a salesman to explain the technique he used to sell a one-million-dollar policy. "Friends," he began, "I went by the book. When I got to his office, knowing what sticklers doctors are, I made sure to arrive on the dot for our appointment. I found the place jammed. I waited four hours to see him, and he appreciated it. He told me how it pleased him to meet a salesman who knows how to conduct himself in a professional man's office. I smiled warmly, let him know that was quite all right, and used this cue to ask him about himself. I listened attentively to every word, going out of my way to agree with the wonderful opinion he had of himself. He talked three hours and then asked me to come back. I returned the next week, went through the same procedures, made the sale, and when I left his office, I knew I had made a friend for life." Then, after a pause, he concluded, "But boy! What an enemy he made."

Friendship also involves taking some calculated risks; anything worthwhile does. Life is full of calculated risks. People can hurt me. For example, a diver stands poised on the high board. He plunges

toward the water knowing he might possibly mis-
calculate with a potential back injury as the result.
But he figures the risk and goes ahead and dives. I
have no guarantee that friendliness will make
friendship happen. It may not. But if it does,
something new and rich and humanizing begins to
take shape between me and other people.

Muriel James and Lois M. Sabary in their book,
The Heart of Friendship, tell how Ben Franklin
and a number of his most ingenious acquaintances
formed "a club of mutual improvement" which
they called the "Junto." Every Friday night the
group of friends met to discuss points of morals,
politics, or philosophy. The Junto Club met for
almost four decades and, in Franklin's words,
"was the best school of philosophy, morality, and
politics that then existed in the province." Members inspired each other to read, write, and speak
in public. They became excellent scholars and
speakers while remaining close friends without in-
terruption for forty years.

Yet, I have found that when I make friends, I do
not avoid conflict. My ego often collides with the
ego of my friend. Furthermore, my friends are not
always friends of each other. People do not stop
creating conflicts simply because they become
friends. Friends get angry with each other as well
as with enemies. And I treat friendship unfairly if I
overlook these problems.

Anger has a role to play in friendship. My friends have qualities I admire, and I look to them for support. Yet, precisely because we know each other better, I will probably disappoint my friends more than their casual acquaintances.

My wife is my lover and my friend. I don't know how many times she has carefully explained to me what she likes and what she doesn't like about my behavior. All too often I do what I feel like doing anyway. Finally, when she's had it, she tells me! Thank God. Among friends that's far better and more creative than the silent treatment of hurt feelings.

Of course, if I bring nothing to the relationship but anger, friends quickly drift away. Anger has its limits and I need to learn them. So, friends develop ways of knowing how far to go and when to stop. Martin E. Marty in an article entitled "Friendship Tested," comments, "Friends have more motives for ending anger than for continuing it; their friendship constitutes a better basis for building on trying experiences than for letting them shatter relationships . . . the curious joining of anger and friendly love offers alternatives in a world of hatreds."*

Still, I don't see friendship as simply one more

*From *Christian Century*, Dec. 24, 1980, p. 1267.

combat zone in the battle of life. Of course, people who care deeply about anything will disagree. And yes, when friends argue, they run the risk of losing their friendship. Only God knows how many former friendships ended in a generation-long feud.

Yet friendship gives me a tool with which to deal creatively with conflict. Trying to suppress conflict is like trying to hide TNT in my basement. Sooner or later it will blow up. How much better to anticipate disagreement and work at ways to handle it. Humor helps. And friends can tell by the tone in the other's voice when they've gone far enough. They have in a way decided not to let anything break their friendship. They treat arguments the way they treat a game of bridge. It is just a game, no matter how seriously they take it while playing. So friendship gives me room to develop my own integrity and values through wrestling with other people with different ideas and values.

At a still deeper level, I have to believe in people to make friends. I know people can fool me. I'm not arguing for blindness or stupidity. Yet I've seen people come back to life when they feel someone believes in them.

I heard of an inner city minister who passed a cigar store every day on his way to church. Each day he noticed a man slouched in the doorway, dispirited and apparently beaten. Everything about him bothered the conscience of this good preacher. One day, he doesn't know why he did it, he reached in his pocket, pulled out two loose dollar bills, pressed them into the man's hand, and whispered to him, "Don't despair." The next day as the preacher went past the cigar store, the man lurched forward and pressed sixteen dollars into his hand. "What does this mean?" asked the astonished preacher.

"It means 'Don't Despair' won the fourth at Santa Anita and paid eight to one," the man answered. Obviously, the preacher's act of kindness in this instance was misplaced. But it is far better to have that happen than to miss an opportunity to give encouragement.

Most of us need encouragement. We need someone to say, "Don't despair," to us. I need a friend who believes in me. Of course, I need someone whose faith in me goes beyond a couple of bucks and a cheery word. And yet what a positive effect just two words can have. "Don't despair." For a fleeting moment I feel like somebody cares about me. In such a moment all my curses on humanity and its inhumanity dissolve in tears of gratitude. I come to a turning point in my life. When that kind of faith gets loose, it puts heart into people. Along comes a teacher who challenges me to try something I thought I could never do. That teacher believed in my ability, and I did it.

Faith, that's the keystone in the arch of friendship. I can't ultimately be happy with a friend I do not believe in. Faith in people carries me out of myself and transforms my impoverished solitary *I* into an enriched sense of *We*. I am not whole by myself; those in whom I believe are the rest of me.

Friends light up my life like the sun. I need people who make me do what I can. Friends do this for me. Mrs. Browning asked Charles Kingsley, "What is the secret of your life? Tell me so I can make my life beautiful, too."

And Kingsley said, "I had a friend."

But friendship has even deeper meanings. When I get discouraged about the evil, shameful ways human beings behave, where can I go to regain my faith that humanity is worthwhile? To my friends! To that piece of humanity I do believe in. To that little fragment of the race I find beautiful to know and easy to love. Friendship becomes a hot house where a confident faith in human worth can get a start which later I can transplant in a wilder, colder, more foreboding world. Sooner or later a time comes when we just can't go on believing in humanity and working for the common good unless we have some fine friendship at the center of our lives.

What else has the power to lift humanity up and create in people the very quality it wants to love there? I can't ask people to be worthy of my love before I befriend them. I must befriend people first in order to make them worth loving at all. I

don't know how we can do that without friends.
It's easier to love humanity in and through and
because of them.

In one sense we don't know anything about a
friendly world. We never had one. Yet at the center of my life, in a few relationships I know what
friendship is. It's the most beautiful and right way
of living people can experience. I can't shake the
feeling that all people in all their relationships are
made to live this way. I need these few great friendships at the center of my life to go on believing in
people.

This world offers a great many people to believe
in. Of all the great issues of our complex time this
may be the greatest. We began our century with
such great faith. It was shallow and mistaken at
many points, but still we believed we could move
ahead. But the great Depression followed close on
the heels of the first World War and then came the
second World War, followed by the Cold War and
now scarcity. And I feel an almost complete rever-
sal of mood. Today a great fog of cynicism has
settled over the common mind, and with it a paralysis of hope and creative energy. People get misled
into believing, "What's the use? You can't change
human nature. People will go on being selfish forever. You can't break the blind self-absorption of
nations."

But what an opportunity! Yes, we live in a time

full of cynicism and doubt with people caught in embarrassing circumstances. Yet all of that is just like dry fuel waiting for the lightning of friendship and faith to strike and set it afire.

So I have to dare to tell people the warm feelings I have about them. I hear a lot of talk that our culture does not allow men to express their feelings. I don't like the caricature of the average man as someone so choked with ambition that he can't relate to other people. This stereotyped, success-oriented male sees his family as consumers of his productive power and other people as important only if they hinder or advance his career.

But I have a hard time fitting my men friends into that caricature. I remember Steve agonizing about how to advance his career without losing his integrity. I remember Jim agonizing about leaving a promising engineering career to work with juveniles in the probation department. I remember Bob continually passed over for promotion, yet steadily working away.

I hear a lot of dumb talk about men hiding their feelings and not knowing how to express them. I don't believe it for a minute. People who say men are uncommunicative simply don't know how to listen to men. Many men did not grow up in the "feely-touchy" school of expression. This school teaches that feelings must be expressed by hugs or tears or shouts to be genuine. Why then, over a cup of coffee or when I worked with them in the factory or on a construction site or sat with them in a committee meeting, have I listened to so many men tell me straight out exactly how they felt? Simply listening to such frank expression of feeling gives friendship a chance.

Maybe you have never wondered why geese fly along in V-formation when they head south. Why don't they fly in a cluster? Two aerodynamic engineers wondered about it and set up a wind tunnel experiment to find out. They discovered that as each bird flaps his wings it creates an uplift for the bird that follows. By flying in V-formation the whole flock has 71 percent greater flying range than if each bird flew on his own. When a bird falls out of the formation, he feels the extra weight of trying to go it alone.

Of course, I have to live my own life, but I do that best in relation to my friends. My friends chide me and point out my faults to me, but they defend me in public. When I make a fool of myself, they believe I haven't done a permanent job. And maybe when all is said and done, the best we can ever be is a friend.

Jesus specialized in friendship. He put himself into people. He touched them. And these people touched others, and then others still. And so he went, working forever. Within the general body of his followers he picked twelve men "as his companions" (Mark 3:14). He made them his friends. And within this inner circle was a more intimate circle still—Peter and James and John. Those three alone went with him to the Mount of Transfiguration when he prayed in triumph, and those three alone went with him in the Garden of Gethsemane when he prayed in grief. They were his special friends. No one in the world today would remember much of what Jesus said or did if it were not for those friends of his and the message they gave us. Jesus did all of his work through friendship.

The more I think about Jesus' last week before the crucifixion, the more my mind centers not on the crowd but on that inner circle, so fallible, so frightened, yet at heart so true, on whom everything that Jesus had done depended and into whose faces he looked that last night to say, "I call you servants no longer . . . I have called you friends" (John 15:15). Jesus' last week is, I think, the most alluring study in friendship that history records.

How much that inner circle of friends meant to Jesus as he rendered to the whole world his supreme service. His friends helped sustain him. With hostility surrounding him and suffering waiting for him, he drew close to his friends. He had never talked to them before as he did that last night. And just before they said good-by, he looked into their faces and said, "There is no greater love than this, that a man should lay down his life for his friends. You are my friends . . ." (John 15:13–14).

Here's the point. No relationship in human life matters much unless it blossoms into friendship. That's the truth. Many relationships give us the chance for friendship, but they are often worse than nothing unless friendship comes. Father and daughter, mother and son, what beautiful relationships. Yet some people don't find them so—not unless they become friendship. Is there anyone who finds life so easy that he or she has no needs which friendship alone can meet?

No wonder Jesus actually described the object of the giving of his life in terms of his friends. Of course he gave his life for the whole world. And yet, on the very eve of his crucifixion Jesus put it quite differently. He said he would lay down his life for his friends. And I think I know why. Suddenly, there is something about him that brings him very close to me. Sometimes, when I am discouraged about humanity, when I can't work up much enthusiasm to sacrifice myself for this sorry humankind, where do I go to reestablish my confidence in humanity and that it's worth working for? To my friends! To those people I do believe in. To that little fragment of the race I find beautiful to know and easy to love! I go to them and come back

again feeling reassured that humanity is worth
working with and for.

During the Second World War a Dutch sailor
floated in the South Atlantic in a rubber raft for
thirty-eight days. He survived without food and
water after the first few days. The intense heat of
the tropical sun just about dried him out. Sharks
followed the raft day after day. He had a fear of
falling asleep and being dragged by them into the
deep. But after his rescue his greatest joy was not
getting out of the sun or away from the sharks or
getting food or water. At first he couldn't talk because of his weakness; he just listened. But when
he could talk, he said, "I never before realized
that people are so important to us." When we realize our interdependence, our need for friendship,
we take a big step toward a fuller life. As I develop
the art of friendship, I begin to appreciate the
human longings of others and overlook the weak-
nesses, as I hope they will overlook mine.

How do we keep from growing old inside? The
only way I know to make friends with time is to stay
friends with people.

In one of his columns in *Christian Century*,
Martin Marty quotes Robert MacAfee Brown: "If I
tried to deal with time by myself I would lose abso-
lutely. Of that I am certain. And I who tend in-
stinctively to be more of a 'private person' than a
'public person' need to keep reminding myself of

this . . . taking community (or friendship) seriously, not only gives us the companionship we need, it also relieves us of a notion that we are indispensable. What a gift! It is immensely liberating to discover that the world and its future will not depend exclusively on us. Others, too, can be allowed to help redeem the times."

*Quoted from *Creative Dislocation: The Movement of Grace*, © 1980 by Abingdon.

9

Your

Money

and Your

Life

IN A WELL-REMEMBERED ROUTINE JACK BENNY stands at the mercy of a holdup man. The man shouts, "Your money or your life."

No response from Benny.

He shouts again, "Your money or your life."

Benny, his hand to the side of his face, finally replies, "I'm thinking, I'm thinking."

Money matters. The current great American inflation began in early 1965. The only thing that comes down now is rain. And that soaks you. Money won't go as far as it used to, but it goes faster. One man said, "I made more money this year than I could afford." Pollster George Gallup calls infla-

143

tion America's biggest concern. "Money talks." Sometimes I agree with a friend who answers, "Yeah, and all mine ever says is 'good-by.'"

Worse yet, inflation or recession can radically affect my feeling of self-worth and my overall sense of trust or mistrust of life. Fathers can become insecure about themselves as providers, and mothers, yearning to expand their interests, become more homebound, while children (with their naturally shaky self-images) find identity "through the brands of jeans whose price is beyond their reach."

Besides, it feels like whatever solutions emerge will have to go beyond "big business" or "big government." Money-anxiety can keep me from getting the perspective I need. Money-anxiety grows out of endless worrying about whether I can get enough goods to give me security. Will inflation or recession take them away? Suppose I lose my job tomorrow. Money, real estate, investments in gold, whisper promises in my ear which they can never fulfill. Cash in the bank promises to save me from anxiety but it never does. Someone once asked John D. Rockefeller, Sr., how much money he thought would be enough. He answered, "Just a little bit more."

Roger Hickey of the National Center for Economic Alternatives notes that the inflation of the last decade has been especially demoralizing because it has affected necessities far more than the general rise in the consumer price index reflects. "There are expenditures that can't be put off," Hickey says. "What all this means is that for the first time the middle-class family is seeing the American Dream turning back on itself. The expectation that next year will be better than last year, of a better life for your kids, has been bitterly disappointed. The future is looking worse."

So I see no easy or simple solution to money matters. Americans have not yet reached a national consensus on who's to blame for inflation or recession. Probably to the end of time most people will want or actually need more than they have. So how do two people who love each other come to grips with money matters?

I used to think of money as a reward for work done. Actually, humanity invented money for convenience but not for enslavement. Two people who love each other can make money a tool to bring happiness if they agree on what makes them happy and how much it costs. Hoover Rupert in an article entitled "The Green Grass Across the Fence" tells of an American auto dealer who had problems. His business went into a terrific slump. In fact, he went bankrupt when foreign-import compact cars took over the field. His wife divorced him. His kids denied his relationship to them. He started drinking and became a bum on the streets. One day he walked down an alley looking for a little wine left in a bottle. He found one with a cork in it. He pulled out the cork and a genie popped out of the bottle. The genie thanked the ex-auto dealer profusely for rescuing her. "For your act I will grant you one wish." The man thought: Foreign car dealers are making all the big money nowadays. So he said, "My wish is to be a foreign car dealer in a major city." When he awoke he found he had become a Chrysler dealer in Tokyo!

What a nightmare when you consider the recent financial troubles at Chrysler, plus the impossibility of finding much of a market for the big car in Tokyo. Yet it shows how often I dream of something that will make me happy. But when I get it, I am no better off than I was, and sometimes I'm a great deal worse off.

People use money in ways that reveal how they feel about basic things, including power, authority, love, acceptance, superiority, inferiority, and so on. How important then to find out how people who love each other feel about money. After all, responsibility to one's family is first and foremost emotional, not financial.

What does it matter if we gain a house and become a mortgage slave? I've found a dirty little secret about real estate. People who own valuable houses that have tripled in value in six years are scared. They haven't taken their profits, and they probably never will. They can't cash in for two reasons: first, they don't want to pay capital gains taxes, and second, if they sell their valuable house and take the profits what are they going to do? Rent?

James K. Glassman, in an article entitled "Prisoners of Real Estate" tells of a friend who is a reporter for the *Washington Star*. He has made sacrifices. He and his wife, who works for the Food and Drug Administration, make about $50,000 a year between them. In 1974 they bought a house in Cleveland Park for $40,000. They sold it for $70,000 and parlayed the profits into a Capitol Hill Townhouse for $150,000. Now they have traded up again into the big time—Georgetown—for $260,000 with $160,000 mortgage at 14 percent. Their payments are $2,000 a month, leaving them about $150 a week to live on after taxes. "We eat a lot of chicken salad sandwiches," says the reporter, "and we've decided we can't afford kids for awhile. But we think what we're doing is important."

But even deeper than that, what difference does it make? What if dad keeps getting great promotions for the sake of his family and in the process sacrifices his integrity? Money just gets mixed up in everything. And I don't know who can escape it very easily. I can say I don't love money—that I love my wife and family more than anything on earth. I wanted good housing and good food and good clothes and a good education for my children. But I can't get food and clothes or housing or education for nothing. I have to pay for them. And I often have to pay through the nose.

So love of my family gets all mixed up with love of money. The best and the worst in me mix and get out of focus. My feelings about money can harden my heart and soften my head. So to begin with, I have to find out what money means to me emotionally. How do I feel about it? Can I remember times when as a child I had to pay for money with affection I didn't feel for the other person at the time? Can I remember when I didn't get my allowance as punishment for something that had nothing to do with my having that money?

Have I ever treated money as an end in itself, rather than a means? On the other hand, you may have seen your father or mother spend money like a drunken sailor and felt there wouldn't be any for an emergency or a big celebration. Maybe you watched one parent spend all the family money. You saw one parent use money like a club, smashing any real feeling of working together between the parents.

And, of course, as a child I remember church people calling money "filthy lucre." They seemed to see it as a necessary tool to survive on earth but not something you should talk much about.

So money gets all mixed up with feeling loved or approved or rewarded. Clearly, until I sort out my feelings about money, I can make big bad mistakes about how to use it in our marriage. For instance, Caroline Bird in her book *The Two Paycheck Marriage* notes that open recognition of the power a wife feels her money earns her has begun a time of trouble in American marriages. Like all other power holders facing challenge, the husband's first reaction is surprise: What am I supposed to do?

For the traditional couple the transition can be especially hard because it is unexpected. Some husbands simply don't know until it has happened, how much they depend on their wives *not* working.

"Working was an economic necessity in our house," a wife wrote about the decision to take a job. "We had five children, over $5,000 in uninsured medical bills with the three youngest boys who seemed to feel oxygen tents and pneumonia were the way every little kid grew up, sporadic periods of unemployment, and a house fire. Our youngest was three. And we were not only flat broke, but way in debt. So going to work seemed the only solution.

"We discussed it. My husband agreed. All seemed fine. Would you believe that the morning I dressed to go for the first day my husband came

completely unglued and spent an hour voicing all
the traditional reasons for not having a working
wife! His male status was being undermined. I was
making him a public embarrassment in front of his
friends and family. I was just planning on finding a
new, richer husband. The whole grim bit. I went to
work anyway. But everything that happened was
because I worked: bad grades, burned hamburger, empty sock drawer, no sex tonight—all
ended up on my door step."

So a husband can feel threatened if he hasn't
cleared up in his own mind the difference between
his wife's current relationship with him and his
mother's domineering one when he was a child.
"Will my wife really act in the punitive way my
mother did?" he must ask himself. The answer is
obviously "No." But he will behave as if the answer were "Yes" unless he gets to the root of his
feelings and brings his feelings into line with present reality.

Money is power. People use money to get things
done. A couple can use that power either to solve
their economic problems or as a club to beat each
other over the head with. Any fool can see where
that leads.

I don't know how a man and a woman can work
out a loving relationship unless they trust each
other. Trust does not mean my wife expects me
always to behave correctly. Trust means she

knows pretty well my intentions and my ethical framework of reference and what I've done in the past. Her trust grows as she knows and understands the emotional hangups I have that make me act the way I do.

One of the first great fights my wife and I had developed over the checkbook of our joint account. Americans fight more over money than any other single thing.

Dr. Eleanor Hamilton in her book *Partners in Love* notes that if the man in a relationship *feels* (without actual data) that the woman in his life will spend their money in ways not his, he simply doesn't trust her. If a woman *feels* (without actual data) that the desires of the man in her life always come first, she may find herself acting like a little girl who has to "please daddy" by paying for his approval with a little sex. She does it to keep him happy so he brings in enough to pay the grocery bill and the mortgage. But that's hardly the same as trusting him and working cooperatively in managing their money matters.

It began to dawn on my wife and me that our love for each other and the management of our money are all wrapped up together. As we began to trust each other more, we could tell each other our fears and work at getting rid of the mindless ones.

I know men who have discovered that their fears about the women they live with have nothing to do with that woman at all. Those fears come from the days when they shuddered over "losing their manhood" as they watched their father go down before a selfish, domineering mother. A woman may discover her fear that when her man comes home with a flashy sports car, it has nothing to do with him and his stability. Her fear comes from her childhood experience of watching her father's excesses.

But men and women are not mind readers. We have to tell each other what troubles us. Together we can take a look at these feelings and see them for what they are. And as we do, we see some of our fears have nothing to do with the present at all.

I think it helps people to discover what my wife and I discovered early in our relationship. As Dr. Hamilton comments, "It doesn't matter who manages the money in your team as long as each of you is represented on the Board of Control and has a voice that is heard and respected by the other."

Millie had worked in a bank and enjoyed keeping books. She's a whiz at a job that bores me limp. She does it better and in half the time that it takes me. But I didn't come to that realization easily. On the other hand, I seem to have some talent in making investments. So Millie doesn't worry too much about that. She keeps the check stubs and pays the bills, and I manage our investments. Of course, these areas overlap and we consult. But here's the important thing. Decide *who* does *what*. When we did that, then we could count on each other to do his or her job.

Next we found we had to establish a budget. Our bills looked huge in comparison to the paycheck. So we worked out a simple budget that represented what we believed important within our means.

That's not always easy. You may have to make a list of things and experiences you think are important in life. The list of a man and the list of a woman may not agree. But if you make a list, it will help you clear up between the two of you what each feels about money matters. If he works hard for a new car and she works equally hard for a trip to Europe, you can count on trouble.

Here's the point: you have to budget emotional values first. Then pool the results, and after that you can put a dollar figure to them.

Of course we all have to pay for certain necessities: food, housing, medical care, and so on. But when a man and a woman know each other's emotional priorities, they have a better chance at coming up with a satisfying financial plan.

People can spend a lot of money on food or very little. But if food comes out high on her list and low on his, they have to compromise.

I like to think I am a rational person. And I am. But I do things because I feel like doing them. In any contest between my feelings and my mind, my feelings usually win. If I do something spectacularly stupid, I will then use my mind to think up clever reasons to explain to my wife why I did this stupid thing. But I do what I do largely because I feel like doing it.

That's why a budget built on emotional values, feelings, translated into terms that my mind can deal with usually works. I don't resent this kind of a budget. This kind of budget represents how we feel and gives us a tool for realizing our deepest desires.

Of course Millie and I didn't budget every penny. Everybody needs a little "mad money." No matter how small our budget, each of us always had a little "mad money" we didn't have to account for.

So how much money do two people need to start life together? Well, two people can get rid of a lot of pressure by consciously deciding to live simply. If people adopt that as an ideal, and not merely as a grim necessity, it can be exciting. All the world pushes on us the hypnotic suggestion that one "must have" certain things to be happy. And if two people begin to total up the price of the "musts," it can strike terror to your soul. Worse yet, I've watched people plunge into a binge of credit-buying that mortgages their lives and their freedom for years ahead.

Thoreau didn't worry about money when he lived at Walden Pond. He discovered that many things which people thought they needed are not necessities at all. People go through life pushing in front of them a house and barn and a hundred acres of land, often making themselves servants to the farm. Of course, Thoreau had it easy in the sense that he didn't marry or have children. But he did make a good point. How easily I'm tempted to increase my material standard of living each year and always keep it ahead of my resources. So, I am panting to catch up, and the very happiness which my possessions ought to provide gets lost in the struggle to pay for them.

Slowly it dawns on me that unless what we own reflects what we really need and our real purposes as well as our ability to pay for them, they become liabilities, not assets. But if we can pay for what we have and if these things reflect what we want, rather than things foisted on us by TV commercials and salesmen of all kinds, we can enjoy them. Now we are spending our money for what we believe in.

Any great venture in life involves taking a calculated risk, and that includes marriage. I've seen so often how quickly ill-health, physical or mental, can crush a young couple. Money matters, and how we use it is a calculated risk as well as one of the privileges of living at close quarters.

So, talk over how you feel about money with the one you love. Work out a money management scheme that fits how you feel; don't settle for one that is foisted on you. Allow each other a little "mad money." Set up your savings and checking accounts and investments in joint names. Agree together that you won't make large expenditures not planned for without mutual consent. Decide who will keep the books and who will think through investments. Don't mortgage your basic goals in life to a standard of living you can't change.

I've watched young couples start out their life together working side by side. They love each other. They get involved in the life of their community and meet new friends. They live a rather simple life because they don't really have much, but they enjoy each other's company. They go for walks on the beach. Then he gets a promotion and six months later, another one, with a sizeable raise. She goes to work to supplement the family income. Suddenly, they feel financially free in a way they never dreamed. Then slowly they begin to notice another kind of stress coming into their lives—another kind of pressure. Why? Because these two dear young people live without any commitment to anything higher than their own enjoyment of life. Sure, they feel some responsibility for the community they live in. They make charitable contributions now and then. But they begin to feel life does consist of the things they possess.

How many possessions are enough? If I have two pairs of shoes, will twelve make me happier? It is so easy for us to try to squeeze more out of the world than there is in it. And even if I own the whole world, it would rattle around inside my soul like a dry pea. Suddenly it dawns on me: it's not an issue of whether I'm going to be good or bad or selfish or generous. The question is whether or not I'm going to let the good things of this world make a fool of me.

I've watched people save their dollars and lose their lives. Oh, they still go on living and breathing, but Life with a capital "L"?—hardly. I remember a smalltown weekly newspaper which reported on the robbery and murder of a local businessman. Muggers had attacked him on the way home from his store the previous Saturday night. The newspaper reported, "But fortunately for the deceased, he had just deposited his day's receipts in the bank, with the result that he lost nothing but his life."

Imagine! Nothing to lose but our lives! Years ago a hardheaded journalist wrote, "It is a good thing to have money and the things that money can buy, but it is a good thing to check up once in awhile and make sure you have not lost the things money cannot buy."

When John Calvin died, the reigning Pope, Pius IV, commented: "The power of that heretic lay in the fact that he was indifferent to money." Exactly! How easy for a person to die rich if he's content to live miserably. The ability to make money is an isolated talent, like being able to wiggle your ears, and deserves no more praise or blame than this. Some people seem naturally gifted to turn one penny into two: others are remarkably consistent at losing the first penny.

I've read more nonsense on making money than any other subject in the world except making love. All the platitudes don't mean a thing: perseverance and honest toil will not make you rich; dishonesty is as likely to land you in prison as in a penthouse.

Of this I am reasonably sure: if you want money badly enough, if you want it more than anything else in the world and to the exclusion of everything else in the world, you will get it. Money-makers have this in common, an intense desire for money as an end in itself. They dedicate themselves to a cause, and when you combine this dedication with the peculiar talent for acquisition of material things, you can't miss.

It's as futile for people like me to try to get rich as it is for an armless man to play the piano. Frustration and misery wait for those whose ambition exceeds their ability. The only smart thing for me to do is dedicate myself to other values and find happiness in them.

Jesus said something that helps me at this point.

"Do not store up for yourselves treasures on earth, where it grows rusty and moth-eaten, and thieves break in to steal it. Store up treasure in heaven. . . . For where your treasure is, there will your heart be also . . . you cannot serve God and Money" (Matt. 6:19–21, 24).

To begin with, he seems to attack the idea of money as security. What my broker sells, he calls "securities." By "securities" he means stocks and bonds. He spells security with the letters I-N-V-E-S-T-M-E-N-T.

My insurance agent has the same idea. A young couple says, "We may not be rich, but we're secure," as they gaze lovingly at their new policy. They've insured the house, the car, their lives. Life insurance seems the ultimate security, since death is the ultimate insecurity. Of course the Bible urges me to save money. Brokers and insurance salesmen act as God's servants as they help me to do this.

Yet the thought of death points me to a kind of security more important than life insurance. Suddenly Jesus' words seem very personal. "Art, you cannot serve God and money." But for a long time I tried to do just that. I served God but not in so bigoted a fashion that it would interfere with my trying to squeeze out of this world all the good things I could. Of course, I don't believe a conflict exists between a reasonable enjoyment of life in this world and faith in the world to come. But

sooner or later we all come to a moment of truth—
a moment when we have to choose either the things
we can see or the things we can't see, either God or
money. One or the other of these is finally and
decisively important. It can't be both.

So I began asking myself questions like, "If my
house caught fire last night and I had time to rescue only one thing, what would it have been?

(a) a package of government bonds, unknown to the
tax man and uninsured?
(b) an original picture of great beauty, fully insured?
(c) a Bible passed down for generations in the
family?

Which would I really choose?

I have a streak of Mammon in me. And it doesn't
go well with faith in God. Even on my way to the
altar of God, I can burn a candle at the altar of
Mammon, or I can burn a candle at the altar of
God on my way to worship Mammon. If only I
could worship both, it would be fine. But I have to
choose. That basic loyalty may only become clear
in moments of crisis, but it determines the whole
set and direction of my life.

The earlier in life I learn that lesson, the more
content I'll be. Not having to concentrate on ava-
rice any more, I can free myself to concentrate on
the pursuit of truth, beauty, love, friendship, and
the other encouragements of human life.

10

How

to Keep

Your

Spirit Up

WHO CAN ARRANGE LIFE PERFECTLY? I CAN'T.
God knows I try. I make plans, but suddenly my
feet go out from under me, and I take a spectacular
fall, and my spirits sink. When they do, I remember a whole spiritual dimension of life I'd half forgotten. I say half forgotten because every time I
hear, "He gave a spirited talk," or "She's a spirited girl," I sense some such dimension exists.

A young woman in her mid twenties complained
to her counselor that she felt nervous and depressed because life had grown so hectic: too many
big weekends, too many discos, too many late
hours, too much talk, too much wine, too much
"pot," too much love-making.

"Why don't you stop?" the therapist asked, mildly. Her patient stared blankly for a moment, and then her face lit up: "You mean I really don't have to do what I want to do?"

So many of us want to live our own lives, be our own judges, our own creators, our own saviors— yet the more we make ourselves absolute and independent, the more lonely and frustrated we become. Kenneth Boulding notes in *Beasts, Ballads and Bouldingisms*, "The real name of the devil is *suboptimization*, finding out the best way to do something that should not be done at all. The engineers, the military, the government, and the corporations are all quite busy at this." And so am I. It's so easy to do something interesting rather than something important.

Yet people living at close quarters stand on the threshold of a great spiritual adventure. The infant is filled as he sucks a nipple. The one-year-old is fulfilled as he walks. The two-year-old feels good when he shouts, "No." The sixteen-year-old feels fulfilled as he gets a date for the prom. In adult life fulfilling things take more thought to figure out. Some needs are satisfied, and others arise as we move through life. Picking up the pieces of one's unfilled hopes and dreams can make every stage of life a high adventure.

I've traced with you some guidelines for living at close quarters. They aren't rules. I look at them more as exercises in maturity. Some underline "conserving" what you have, and passing it along. And some emphasize "the progressive"—moving beyond where you are. Not all apply to everyone. Choose areas of your own special need. With regular exercise, healthy personality traits get built right into your psyche and become as natural for you as speaking English or writing righthanded. But when a man and woman cross the threshold of life together, a deeper level of living opens for the two of them.

Our spiritual life is the only precious thing we possess. Yet it's so fragile. Never before have people had to so carefully guard a little clear space at the center of their lives in which this tender flame can continue to burn. The deepest things in life always go beyond explanation. I can't explain why great music will move me to tears. Great artists simply cannot explain their art. And who can explain the overwhelming emotional and spiritual experience of human love? Why should anyone need to make it sound like the simplest thing in the world?

But just because there is profound mystery involved in human spirituality does not mean that it is obscure. Like most of the important things in my life what I mean by spiritual I find hard to describe. I have a hard time telling someone else what I mean by such simple basic things as love or beauty or truth, but I can't get along without any of them. Still my inability to define them does not mean I have not in some sense experienced the reality of them. I can explain what I mean by a typewriter far easier than I can explain what I mean by love. But I can get along without a typewriter, whereas I can't get along very long without loving and feeling loved.

It's the unessential things I find easiest to define. Life offers great moments that give me flashes of insight into this spiritual dimension of my experience. These are once in a lifetime kind of moments, like the birth of a child. Suddenly I catch a glimpse of the meaning at the heart of the mystery of life. Such moments give direction and substance. They lift me above the other moments of life that bring fear and terror and anxiety.

I remember boarding a plane at 11:45 A.M. at Kennedy Airport to fly to the west coast. About six minutes into the air a terrific bang in the back of the plane shook the whole aircraft. The captain's voice came on the intercom very calmly, "Ladies and gentlemen, nothing to be alarmed about, we have a minor compression problem in one engine." In spite of his soothing words I sat very light. I had trouble believing it was possible to have a "minor" problem with an engine. We kept going for a few minutes until another terrific bang shook the whole plane. The captain's voice came on again saying, "We're shutting down the engine and have headed back to Kennedy." In spite of his words the next few minutes dragged by filled with terror. We did land safely and stayed on the ground about six hours. Finally the airline rounded up another aircraft, and we took off again about 6:00 P.M. into a gray, overcast, rainy sky. Everybody on board felt anxious. But we went up smooth as glass—up through the clouds. And then at about 20,000 feet we began to level off. The moon was out and I could see the stars. It was a glorious evening. I looked down and saw the lights of the countryside below. Suddenly the anxiety and the fear and the gloom I had known began to fade. I was lifted up into another view of life, into another world.

We all need moments like that to lift us above the anxiety and the depression of daily living. We need to catch a glimpse of the light of another world.

The pressures of life at close quarters, the everydayness of it, the meeting of people, answering the phone, writing the letters, keeping the appointments, wear people down. It never seems to let up. And yet every now and then like a flash of lightning against a dark sky people do catch a glimpse of another world. We catch a glimpse of the reality of a spiritual dimension.

I've known young people who have lived on the concrete sidewalks in the center of our Los Angeles area. They've grown up and lived in decrepit and decaying housing. They know that world and they see it every day. And then one day they see someone selling roses on a street corner. They've never seen a rose grow up through the sidewalk in front of their housing development.

Then suddenly a year or two later they round the corner several miles from their home and see the Pacific Ocean. They had not known it was there. They never saw it before. Out in the distance an ocean liner goes by. Suddenly these young people understand that there's more to life than they had seen. Life has more to offer than concrete pavements and decrepit housing. They have suddenly caught sight of a whole other world. All of us who live at close quarters stand on the threshold of just such moments. We need such moments!

How easily we can simply live life on one level—the ground level, not architecturally, but spiritually. We can dismiss a spiritual dimension altogether. Yet if we do we have no attic or no cellar. There's nothing to stand in awe of. Woe to the man or woman who become so familiar with each other that they no longer stand in awe of the other person.

The absence of this spiritual understanding of life poisons our time. At the close of his Harvard address, Alexander Solzhenitsyn said, "If the world has not come to its end, it has approached a major turn in history, equal in importance to the turn from the Middle Ages to the Renaissance. It will exact from us a spiritual upsurge, we shall have to rise to a new height or vision, to a new level of life where our physical nature will not be cursed as in the Middle Ages, but even more importantly, our spiritual being will not be trampled upon as in the Modern era.

"This ascension will be similiar to climbing onto the next anthropologic stage. No one on earth has any other way left but—upward."

Maybe a good many people thought they could get along pretty well by ignoring this spiritual dimension. But can my eyes get along pretty well without light? Can my lungs get along pretty well without air, or my heart pretty well without love? If they can, then I might be able to get along pretty well by ignoring the spiritual nature of my being.

Many of us reached adulthood with a ready-made set of answers to both religious and ethical questions. We simply inherited them from our father or mother. But frankly, we didn't have time for sterile church fights and the numbing boredom of worship as usual. We got tired of the old-time-sit-down-keep-quiet religion. Yet we find it hard to keep our spirits up without opening the inner doors of our spiritual awareness and committing ourselves to a life-long search for truth of the spirit. And besides many of us arrive at adulthood with spiritual concepts at a third-grade level. But those

third-grade ideas don't do us a lot of good. They
don't fit reality as we know it today.

A former Roman Catholic priest, James Ka-
vanaugh, writes: "I lost my God, the one whose
name I had known since childhood. I knew his
temper, his sullen rage, his ritual of forgiveness. I
knew the strength of his arm, the sound of his
insistent voice and I never told him how he frightened me, how he followed me as a child when I
begged for candy on Halloween. He was a predictable God. I was the unpredictable one. He was
unchanging, omnipotent, all-seeing. I was volatile
and helpless. Now my easy God is gone. He knew
too much to be real. He talked too much to listen.
He knew my words before I spoke them; but I also
knew his answers as well—computerized and turned
into dogma. He's gone—my easy, stuffy God."

This means that I have to quit believing we
"give" religion to our children. At best, adults can
help children discover their own. In fact, religious
dogma can prove a substitute for direct spiritual
experience, and religious observance can be
thought of as a way to buy spiritual grace.

For example, if someone doesn't eat ham, does
he or she gain spiritual strength from thinking of
an ancestor's foresight at a time when pork was
likely to be contaminated and dirty? Or does the
act simply reflect an emotional fear masked as "religious observance"?

According to Nicolas Berdyaev: "There is no longer room in the world for a merely external form of Christianity, based on custom. The world is entering upon a period of catastrophe and crisis, when we are being forced to take sides, and in which a higher and more intensive spiritual life will be demanded of Christians."

A commitment to a lifelong search for truth of the spirit is surely one of humanity's greatest adventures. Unfortunately, many marriages get stuck at the level of ready-made religious answers handed down to each one of the persons in the relationship. People confuse emerging spiritual reality with simply keeping prescribed religious rituals. Because of this confusion many men and women fail to see their capacity to join hearts in a search that could light up their lives.

What should people living at close quarters do about pressure from their own respective religions to act in ways contrary to their own convictions? An important question!

Suppose you find yourself in an authoritarian religious community that claims the power to control your private and personal behavior even though you have not yourself submitted voluntarily. Years ago in New England anyone who didn't belong to the village church had to pay a fine. That attitude, unfortunately, still lives in some religious communities.

Ideally, a church exists to help people discover the reality of God and develop as spiritual persons in the light of that revelation. Other people who share that faith give emotional support to the emerging spirituality. And most of us need all the support we can get. If a church fellowship raises my self-esteem—if people care enough to lift each other out of the swamp of failure, then it makes an incalculable contribution to human life on earth. Almost everybody needs help at one time or another. And because we do, we have an obligation to take a hand in giving it. People have found that belonging to a church is one way to do this.

If you and your mate decide to join such a fellowship, do it with enthusiasm, remembering that the people in it have all the frailties and foibles of normal human beings. And yet, with them, you may discover you share responsibility for creating a spiritual body that can have a profound effect upon the spirit of the community where you live.

And I've found this thought helpful. Ministers and rabbis and priests don't exist as servants of the congregation or the conscience of the community. He or she has studied for years the thought and practice of a particular community of faith, but they don't exist to control how you think in an authoritarian way. At least they shouldn't. Rather, such people can point to spiritual truth they have discovered and say, "This I believe. Now what do you think?"

So, I believe that people at close quarters can create space to talk over their own feelings about the meaning of life. Why keep silent before what we think of as imponderables? All of us at one time or another, in one way or another ask ourselves, "Who do you think God is?" Yet I find people often afraid to tell the one they love most what they think at such a level.

Dare to open your minds to the imponderables. Believe in your ability to receive spiritual truth. Preachers have no monopoly on spiritual truth. If you keep at it, I believe you will find yourself moving from playing with ideas about God to an experience of God himself. God and ideas about God are not the same. You may find yourself saying, "Dear God, you brought me into existence. You understand my limitations, my moods, my feelings, my instincts. You are responsible for me. I live in response to you." That's the difference between talking about God and talking with God. It's the difference between a boy passing a note in the classroom that says "John loves Mary" and walking up to her and saying, "Mary, I love you."

Sometimes I ask myself, "How much of my faith is memory?" Bible stories? Favorite hymns? How much of my own faith gathers around some bright moments when God seemed very real to me? Such memories matter. A large part of real religion is memory. But God help us if we get locked into a religion that is nothing but memories.

If one of the apostles got loose in one of our churches today I think he might ask us: "Don't tell me about your memories, what about your faith now—your present contact with God, your living trust in Christ, your spontaneous joy in the things you believe?" And then he might explain how once he and the other disciples had been living precariously on the memory of Jesus. Even the resurrection of Jesus had begun to become a distant event, something they looked back to with wonder and reverence. And then suddenly the Spirit came and they no longer knew God as a remote Creator and Ruler but as a living present power. Jesus no longer remained a memory but actually came alive within them and among them. They no longer simply celebrated the fact of his resurrection but they had the assurance of his daily companionship. The dead bones of theology came to life as a working religion.

The only way anyone ever tests or verifies the reality of God is by direct personal experience. No one has to remain forever hung up on questions about God. The God of personal discovery may not fit our preconceived prejudices and assumptions of who God should be or what God should do. Suddenly God becomes no longer a God according to me but God according to God.

Such spiritual reality dawns on people. No one can preach it into them. No one can argue it into them. I have five senses with which I relate to the physical world. I have a sense of sight, a sense of smell, a sense of taste, a sense of hearing, and a sense of touch. By these senses I go out into the world and the world comes into me. But I also have a sixth sense. Sometimes I come home at night and have only to open the door to sense something's wrong. The house looks the same, but I know something's wrong. Or sometimes when I've worked with a group of people on a particular plan I sense I have messed up the plan. I messed it up not because I broke any law or did anything wrong. I just sense it. At other times I sense I have done exactly the right thing even though most of the people with whom I'm working don't agree with me. I just sense it. It was right. It was true.

Now in somewhat the same way spiritual reality dawns on people. Some call it a sense of God's presence. There is mystery in that, of course. Yet that emerging spiritual reality has powerful effects on human life.

Once my wife and I went to the nursery to pick out a poinsettia plant for Christmas. We wanted to put it right by the front door. But while we were there I noticed that my wife picked up a little Boston fern. I asked, "What are you going to do with that?"

"Well," she said, "the doctor for whom I work had this beautiful Boston fern that shriveled up into a pathetic little plant. I'm going to take this and exchange it for his plant. First of all I'm going to see if he notices (he didn't), but secondly, I'm going to take that pathetic plant of his to our house and see if we can nurse it back to health."

So she brought the plant home from the office. We put it in a place where there was just enough sunlight and just enough moisture. Within days the plant looked stronger, greener, fresher. Something like that happens in people's lives when they are exposed to spiritual reality. New vitality they didn't know existed rises up within them. They find new hope, new courage, new life.

Now, I admit sensing that presence may depend somewhat on the type of person I am. Some people have greater sensitivity to music than other people do. Some people have a greater sensitivity to science and some of us can't see a scientific fact if it stares us in the face. So, I know people who say to me, "Well, Art, you may sense a spiritual reality people call God. But I don't. I wish I could. I honestly want to, but if I'm honest with you, I really don't sense any such presence in this world."

What should my response be? Well, I say, "I believe it." And I say, "I believe" because I can't prove it to them. Yet I believe everyone has a sense of wonder, a sense of awe. I know that some people are color blind or tone deaf. But all of us have some awareness of a mysterious, unutterable beauty loose in creation. All of us have some sense of awe.

Where I am affects my sense of wonder. I know people might discover spiritual reality anywhere at all. But if I'm playing golf and slam my ball off the seventeenth tee into a deep rough, I have a hard time feeling any spiritual reality in that situation. It may be there. Others may feel it. But it's hard for me to pull it off.

But other places affect me quite differently. When I walk out under the clear sky and see the stars, the sheer wonder and magnitude of creation fills me with awe. And other times when I sit with a family and one we all love begins to loose their earthly moorings and slip away, I sense an awesome spiritual reality. Sometimes when I look down into a crib and see a tiny baby, I'm awestruck at the possibility of human life.

And quite frankly, often when I step into a church I am struck with wonder. Without the church I could lose my focus about the nature and the purpose of what I call God. Out under the stars I might feel impressed with the beauty and the power of it all. But if I limit my experience to that sort of place, I could lose the meaning of the mystery. I could get carried away with my emotions out under the stars and become sentimental about spiritual truth and lose any sense of responsibility.

I could miss the meaning and the mystery. I could feel overwhelmed by the power of spiritual reality without ever feeling reassured of the love that never quits and never gets tired and is so graphically portrayed by the cross that hangs in the front of most churches.

People living at close quarters who are searching for spiritual truth will find it dawning on them in surprising places and in surprising ways. It's kind of like when I go to bed at 11:30 P.M. with the room pitch dark. Outside there are just a few glimmers of light. I leave the blinds up. When I wake at 6:30 A.M. I find the room full of light. I don't know when the darkness left and the light came. And even if I had lain awake all night as I sometimes seem to, I would not have felt any dramatic passing of darkness into light. Instead, I would have noticed a gradual development. I would say in the morning, "I went to bed in the dark, but I got up in the light." Or I can go to bed with the blinds drawn tightly, with the room completely dark. I wake up at 6:30 A.M., climb out of bed, and pull up the shade. The sun is blazing. I say, "Here in a moment of time in a conscious act, darkness goes and light comes into the room."

Yes, the spiritual reality of God dawns on our lives in different ways. Sometimes gradually, sometimes all at once. But the light shines on in the darkness and the darkness has never mastered it.

How does God guide us? I'm not suggesting I can safely identify the movement of God's Spirit within me with the upsurging of my unconscious. But I do believe he often works in that sphere. As Vincent Taylor remarks in his book *The Go-Between God*, "We first meet him in the Scriptures hovering over the great depths of chaos, the dragon of the older creation myths, preparing not to bind or eliminate it like Apollo, but to open it up and release what was potential in it. The Spirit is not averse to the elemental world of our dreams, the raw emotion of our fears and angers, the illogical certainties of our intuitions, the uncharted gropings of our agnosticism, the compulsive tides of our history. These are his *milieu*."

God guides me from within. In his book *With God in Red China* Olin Stockwell tells how God led him to write two books during his imprisonment. The idea for the first book came to him in a sudden flash of insight. He went to work on it, and as he worked, he forgot the misery of the prison. But he had barely finished when a second flash came. "This one," he says, "was almost like an electric shock." He felt ordered to write of his prison experience. He protested that he didn't have enough to say, and that if anyone published it, no one would read it. But the inner urging continued.

He continues, "I started in. I have never had so much fun writing anything. I would go to bed at eight in the evening, only to awaken at two in the morning with my mind crowded with memories and stories that could make the day's writing. I would lie there on my cot, waiting impatiently for daylight to come so that I could get released from the burden that was on my mind."

Then he adds, "Please do not misunderstand me. I do not have any private wire to heaven. When my friend Will Shubert used to talk of God's guidance, I listened with the same kind of skepticism with which you may have been reading these words. I was always willing to seek God's advice and then follow my own judgment. And to talk of God's guidance always seemed to me to run into the danger of boasting that you had special access to Headquarters, or to lead you to make independent decisions with little regard for other people's opinions. So I listened to those who talked of God's guidance with a good deal of reservation.

"But not now. I've had too deep an experience and seen a miracle happen that I cannot shrug off. I have learned as I never knew before that tissue-paper thinness of the veil between us and the spiritual world . . . the well of living water is one that never runs dry."

Of course God guides in many ways. He guides us through the wisdom of the Bible. How can I receive more and more of Christ into my soul and feel nourished by him? I find such "soul food" in reading Scripture. "The words which I have spoken to you are both spirit and life," Jesus says (John 6:63). It's in the Bible I read such words. "Your words are words of eternal life," Peter cries (John 6:68). As I read Scripture I hear those words.

And I believe you can discover the presence of the living God standing beside you to see you through your difficulties. If you listen you may hear him saying, "Friend, I know what you are going through; I've been this way before. You may find it difficult, but I'll stand by you and go with you as long as you need me."

I remember how Galileo once said, "The sun which has all those planets revolving about it and depending on it for their orderly functions can ripen a bunch of grapes as if it had nothing else in the world to do." So God can stand with you without deserting the rest of his responsibilities. That may not mean immediate relief, but it does mean ultimate triumph. "Thanks be to God who giveth us the victory!"

And so as we walk through life with the one we love, problems of church background, rites and rituals, become less and less important before the larger issue of an emerging spirituality within us and between us and we look for ways to realize God's presence.